M000310267

Cityscopes are concise, illustrated guides that provide an overview of a city's past as well as a focused eye on its present. Written by authors with unique and intimate knowledge of the cities, each book features a chronological history to the present day. Also including a section of essays on key places or aspects of the city today – from museums to music, public transport to parks, food to fashion – the books offer fascinating vignettes on the quintessential and the quirky, as well as listings of key sites and venues with the authors' own commentaries. Illustrated throughout with contemporary photos and compelling historical images, Cityscopes are essential companions to cities worldwide.

Titles in the series:

Beijing Linda Jaivin

Berlin Joseph Pearson

Buenos Aires Jason Wilson

New York Elizabeth L. Bradley

Paris Adam Roberts

cityscopes

Adam Roberts

PARIS

REAKTION BOOKS

For Patricia, Félix and Jeanne

Published by Reaktion Books Ltd
Unit 32, Waterside
44–48 Wharf Road
London N1 7UX, UK

www.reaktionbooks.co.uk

First published 2017
Copyright © Adam Roberts 2017

Printed and bound in China by 1010 Printing International Ltd

A catalogue record for this book is available from the British Library
ISBN 978 1 78023 746 6

OPENING IMAGES: p. 6: Montmartre steps and the basilica of the Sacré-Coeur; p. 7 (top): view to the Île de la Cité from the Institut du Monde Arabe; p. 7 (bottom): steps of the banks of the Seine; p. 8 (top): night view from Montmartre; p. 8 (bottom): night view of the Centre Pompidou; p. 9 (top): the Tuileries gardens; p. 9 (bottom): the Marais; p. 10 (top): window box in the place de la Contrescarpe; p. 10 (bottom): café terrace at Barbès market; p. 11: pastries at Angelina, rue de Rivoli; p. 12 (top): 'closed for the summer' sign in the rue du Mont Thabor; p. 12 (bottom): relaxing by the canal Saint-Martin; p. 13: Librairie Santon bookshop, passage Verdeau.

Contents

The view from Notre-Dame to the west, including the Petit Pont and the pont Saint-Michel.

Prologue

Paris, a city that has been spared the rebuilds others have had to endure following war and natural disaster, has a living history that is more visible than that of almost any other city in the world. The concentration of historic buildings, the strict municipal planning that has always placed glorious perspectives above functional drabness, and the focus on pleasure and culture, have made it a universal icon of romance.

'Ajoutez deux lettres à Paris: c'est le paradis' (add two letters to Paris and it's paradise), noted the writer Jules Renard in his journal at the end of the nineteenth century. It was a declaration of love to a city that has not been kind to him – his old home on rue du Rocher is now the site of a hulking office block – but also a rather rueful recognition that a piece of the perfection puzzle has always been missing.

For English speakers, Paris would need one more letter for 'paradise', but the rivals from over the Channel or across the Atlantic have always been that little bit more demanding of the city – and indeed envious of its success and influence. And in the City of Light there has always been much to inspire envy.

That has seemingly never been enough, however. Throughout its existence, kings, emperors, presidents and mayors have all been tempted to transform Paris into something else, to add those two – or three – missing letters and create not only a paradise on Earth, but a metropolis that would suitably reflect their own glory.

In the sixteenth century, King François I announced his intention of bringing back the royal court that had deserted Paris and of sprinkling Renaissance magnificence over the city

– a promise he did not keep. Decades later, Henri IV
told suspicious Parisians that he wanted to 'make a whole
world of this city and a wonder of the world'. Even Louis
XIV, who hauled the court out to Versailles, was determined
to turn Paris into the new Rome.

Napoléon Bonaparte was notably scornful of the city's
inhabitants – 'Parisians have always been rebels [*frondeurs*],'
he declared – but he knew the importance of possessing an
imperial city. From his final exile on St Helena, he declared
despairingly that he had dreamed of transforming Paris into
something 'fabulous, colossal, unknown before our times'. It
was a mission that he had had neither the time nor the money
to see to fruition. His nephew Louis-Napoléon came closer
to this ideal, mostly through a paternalistic and sometimes
misguided desire to change the lives of the inhabitants: 'Open
new streets,' he declared, 'clean up the working-class neighbour-
hoods that lack air and daylight, and let the nurturing light
of the sun penetrate everywhere on our walls, like the light of
truth in our hearts.' The country's second emperor demolished
much of the heart of the old city, replacing it with the long,
straight boulevards, the six-storey buildings and the public
parks that remain characteristic of the city today.

Walk through the dusty statue-strewn Tuileries gardens to
the vast place de la Concorde, up the elegant rue Royale to the
Neoclassical Madeleine church, then along the arrow-straight
boulevard Malesherbes to the Byzantine dome of Saint-
Augustin. Turn right there and you will arrive at the home
of Jules Renard. Had he accompanied you, hardly a single
thing would have surprised him, give or take a few shopfronts
and the fact that his house has been crushed by concrete.

Despite a few cosmetic touches, changes in the historic
heart of the city have been almost imperceptible since the
beginning of the twentieth century. 'I see it change like
someone who observes the wrinkles in the corner of the
eyes of a loved one's face each day,' notes the essayist Eric
Hazan, who has spent his entire life exploring the city.

If Hazan still finds beauty in the ageing face of his lifelong
love, he nevertheless appreciates that she has changed in other

ways: 'It is not so much the mineral aspect that has been modified but rather the way in which the city is lived in.' In recent years there has been a smothering sensation that Paris is stagnating. The population of the city has stalled and is ageing; Paris possesses an ever-greater concentration of wealth, but less and less social diversity.

Whereas previous dynasties sought to remodel the city into a terrestrial nirvana, more recent generations have been satisfied with repackaging the past to ever-greater numbers of visitors. 'Each point is a perch for a thousand birds,' declared the writer Jules Romains in 1919, already remarking how dense and crowded a city Paris had become. It is an impression that the millions of tourists who spend hours in queues at the city's principal monuments may share.

Paris is a city of glory, a city of legend, a city of love, but also a city preserved in aspic. As early as 1901 the historian Gabriel Hanotaux wrote of a need to expand the city once again, to add another concentric ring, as Paris had done throughout its history: 'If Paris wants to maintain its position, it must frankly accept its obligations and functions as a great capital, and engage to grow bigger, to open up and to stretch out.'

After decades of a sumptuous but stifling fossilization, Paris is now ready to grow again, notably by finally accepting and incorporating the suburbs it has always shunned but that now dwarf the capital itself. This incarnation has been baptized 'Grand Paris', a rather grandiose name for a metropolis that will probably only ever exist as a bureaucratic institution, but which could nevertheless finally sort out some of the scandalous inequalities in so rich a region.

Whatever happens, Paris will surely continue to attract and inspire. 'One never sees Paris for the first time, one always sees it again,' remarked the Italian writer Edmondo De Amicis in the nineteenth century. It is one of the rare universal cities, a place you feel you know even if you have never visited before, a stateless city that belongs to nobody and to everybody, where love comes and locks itself to bridges. It may not be paradise, but at certain places, at certain angles, at certain times of the day, it comes closer than almost anywhere else in the world.

Rue de Rivoli by the Tuileries gardens, *c.* 1900.

HISTORY

1 Saints and Myths

Walk to the top of the Parc de Belleville in Paris's 20th arrondissement and you will find the best view of the city. Laid out before you – uninterrupted and unobstructed – is Paris's full complexity of towers, domes, rooftops and spires. Rewind 5,000 years and now imagine yourself in the same spot, but this time in the rough footwear of an early traveller who has stopped to rest. Wipe away the monuments and modernity and what will become visible is the exceptional site on which Paris was built.

First of all, there is the river; not the gentle, tightly constrained Seine we know today, but an unruly, sprawling mass of water up to 1 km (5/8 mile) wide, dotted with tiny islands like stepping stones. Stretching away from it is a fast-flowing finger that tickles the feet of the northern hills. Although this branch would later sink into the earth, it lingers damply underground, making unexpected comebacks at times of major flood. Alongside the river are wide plains, sloping gently up towards the hills, that will later provide points of focus and defence for the city. Most of this land is covered in an extremely rich and diverse forest that will provide the material for early construction and the first means of transport. The wood is of such good quality that it will also be exported – along the river – over vast distances. Beneath this landscape is a mineral treasure chest that early visitors are only just beginning to exploit: a rich seam of limestone and gypsum that will later be dug out of the ground over many centuries, leaving the city's famous Swiss cheese subterranean structure. It is the stone that will build the monuments and give the city its uniform colour.

The location is so attractive to visitors today that it is little wonder that this primitive Parisian landscape also proved enticing to weary travellers. Here was water, a safe place to camp, materials for tools, a good climate and abundant animal life to hunt. Crucially, the stepping-stone islands also enabled wanderers to ford the river.

The first to arrive were itinerant hunter-gatherers, who may have passed backwards and forwards across this territory for thousands of years. In several different locations in Paris, archaeologists have uncovered the animal bones they gnawed on – deer and wild boar, even mammoth – and the flint they chipped into weapons around their campfires. Inevitably, people stopped wandering and decided that this was about as good as it would get. Neolithic tribes learned how to plant and cultivate crops, and built camps by the river. In the early 1990s traces of wooden huts and jetties were discovered near the neatly landscaped Parc de Bercy, and several dugout canoes were also miraculously unearthed from an old trace of the river. Later, these early settlers would also use the site's strategic importance to control river traffic and crossings.

The earliest permanent settlers were the Parisii, a Celtic tribe who migrated from beyond the Danube in about 300 BC. The reason for the name they chose for themselves remains a mystery, a matter that would be of little importance were it not for the fact that it spawned the identity of one of the world's most famous cities. Perhaps the most fanciful theory is that the name comes from the mythical Greek prince Paris himself, whose ancestors were said to have settled in the area after the destruction of Troy – although there is no evidence for this theory whatsoever.

Also shrouded in an ancient fog is the name of Lutetia, the Parisii's *oppidum*, or settlement, on the Seine. Some have postulated rather charmingly that it stems from a Gaulish word for mice, but the best guess is that it originated in the Celtic word *luto*, meaning bog or marsh – not a glamorous provenance, but certainly one that fits the topography.

Although the Parisii left no written traces of their own culture, the clues they did leave point to an advanced and progressive community. They produced their own money and controlled trade on a crucial axis on European tin and bronze transportation routes. Archaeological digs have also uncovered tools that show they knew how to make cheese, marking them definitively as early forerunners of the French.

What made the settlement's fortune and prestige, though, also made it a desirable spot to conquer. The Parisii lived in peace and prosperity, but their early bourgeois comforts were brought to an abrupt end by the arrival of the Romans. The community at first turned a deaf ear to the wars breaking out in neighbouring territories, but eventually the Romans forced them into confrontation.

Julius Caesar was the first person to mention the site of Paris in his writings on the Gallic Wars in the first century BC. 'Lutetia', he noted, 'is a town of the Parisii, situated on an island on the river Seine.' Descriptive geographical detail was not the forte of Caesar, who preferred to detail Roman military manoeuvres and endless lists of victories, and accordingly the exact location of this 'island on the river Seine' is still hotly debated. For almost the full extent of the next two millennia, it was thought that it must refer to the Île de la Cité, the centre of today's city and the geographical point zero of France. There is just one small problem with this very reasonable assumption: no traces of pre-Roman occupation have ever been found there.

Wherever the Parisii's *oppidum* was, it was a location for which the Romans were ready to fight. Caesar sent one of his best generals, Titus Labienus, to force the tribe out of its stronghold. Lutetia, peopled by a docile mix of druids, magistrates and traders, had a cruel lack of warriors, but its privileged position on trade routes made it a place worth defending for other neighbouring peoples. An ageing but extremely brave and agile warrior named Camulogene was sent to help defend the territory. Victory for the Roman army was not as rapid as had been hoped, thanks mainly to the cunning and bravery of Camulogene. One of his principal tactics was to use a scorched-earth policy – setting fire to Lutetia and ordering the bridges to be broken down – to hold up the invading army. Once defeat was inevitable, Camulogene waded into the Roman troops, ensuring that he was slain and would never become a prize to be displayed in Rome.

The Romans had won the Battle of Lutetia, but their reward was little more than a few charred huts. If the *oppidum* was no longer in existence, the trade routes were still in place and the name stayed the same. Very slowly the community was rebuilt around the same ancient paths, but Lutetia would almost always be a second-division city for the Romans, who chose to make Lugdunum (Lyon) the capital of Gaul.

The Romans were impressed with the people they found in their new territory, and lumped them all together as Gauls. Nearly all of them, wrote the Roman soldier and historian Ammianus Marcellinus, were 'of a lofty stature, fair, and of ruddy complexion'. Providing perhaps the first example of the French stereotype in history, he also described them as being 'very quarrelsome, and of great pride and insolence'. More positively, he also noted that they were 'exceedingly careful of cleanliness and neatness'.

Roman Lutetia was set up with a typical grid structure that is still visible in Paris today, with the Île de la Cité at its apex. The main route – the *cardo maximus* – followed the ancient north–south path and the river provided an east–west axis. Despite numerous invasions, sackings and rebuilding projects, the route still strikes through the centre of the city today. Later named rue Saint-Jacques, it took on another significance in the Middle Ages as the path through Paris on the Way of St James pilgrimage.

The Romans did all their building on the Île de la Cité and the Left Bank. First came the forum, an obligatory feature in Roman towns of a certain size. It was built alongside the *cardo maximus*, at one of the highest points on the Left Bank (just to the south of today's Sorbonne university). Some 118 m (390 ft) long and 43 m (140 ft) wide, it was the city's administrative centre, but also provided residents with a place to meet, debate and – ever important in Paris – shop.

Lutetia also had an arena (known today as the Arènes de Lutèce), a giant amphitheatre for sporting events, battles and

Uncovered by accident and then promptly largely demolished in the 19th century, the Roman Arènes de Lutèce amphitheatre dates back to the 1st century AD.

theatrical performances. It was built in AD 100 in one of the most attractive spots in the area, near the river and facing the setting sun in order to prolong events as much as possible. It was also one of the largest such constructions in Gaul, and had a capacity greater than the entire population of the city itself. Best preserved of all in Paris today are the thermal baths, which are now part of the city's Musée de Cluny. Unlike the amphitheatre and forum, these have remained in use, albeit in recent centuries as stables, a carriage station or the storeroom of a cooper. The building's 2-m- (6-ft-) thick brick walls ensured its survival, although the medieval Paris home of the bishops of the order of Cluny was curiously later grafted on to one side.

Although the city was of middling size, such facilities were built in Lutetia thanks to a tax levied on its richest inhabitants. Some of the wealthiest belonged to the guild of boatmen (known as the *nautes*), an ancient trade that controlled river traffic and which had also brought Celtic Lutetia its importance. Their wealth and influence in the Roman city was seen most clearly in the Pillier des Nautes, a monumental stone bas-relief that was displayed in one of the city's temples. The Romans had brought their own gods, city-planning and culture, but the Gauls were allowed to keep many of their own traditions, as this 'Pillar of the Boatmen' demonstrated. Featuring both Roman and Celtic gods, it was recovered miraculously in the early eighteenth century during the construction of a crypt in the cathedral of Notre-Dame. Today the impressively sized blocks are displayed in the Musée de Cluny. Although we are sure – by their relative sizes – of the order in which they stood, exactly how they lined up is not clear, making the pillar a kind of primitive Rubik's cube with 64 possible solutions.

The Roman religion that mixed superstition, tradition and borrowed gods largely matched Gaulish beliefs, but these

The frigidarium in the Musée de Cluny is the city's best-preserved Roman edifice.

Roman statue in the frigidarium, possibly representing the Emperor Julian.

were shaken up by the arrival of Christianity in Lutetia. In about AD 250 a wizened old preacher named Denis (who was, some sources claim, 110 years old) arrived in the city with two other evangelists, Rusticus and Eleutherius. The three were said to have been sent by Pope Fabian to convert Gaul to Christianity, but few facts are known about Denis, a figure who would become one of the patron saints of Paris. They passed on their message by preaching secretly in underground quarries around the edges of the city. Their success in converting slaves and other disenfranchised inhabitants drew the attention of the Romans, and they were quickly arrested. At their trial, the preachers were given a choice between submitting to the emperor, thereby renouncing their religion, and death. Denis had no fear of death, though, being fully aware of the message his martyrdom would inspire.

Denis and his two associates were executed on the highest hill in the city, later renamed *mons martyrium* or Montmartre, but this was just the beginning of the legend of St Denis. After being decapitated, Denis was said to have walked several miles with his head tucked under his arm, preaching all the way, before collapsing finally at the point to the north of Paris where the cathedral of Saint-Denis stands today.

The Roman Empire ended its persecution of Christians shortly afterwards, but its grip on Europe was now weakening. For Lutetia, this meant becoming a target for skirmish attacks from the east. Tired of being the victims of pillaging and sabotage, the inhabitants abandoned the Left Bank to set up home on the city's only protected spot, the Île de la Cité.

The Romans' swansong in Paris belongs to Emperor Julian, one of the city's most famous admirers, and the first to put his love for the city down on paper:

> I happened to be in winter quarters at my beloved Lutetia . . . It is a small island lying in the river; a wall entirely surrounds it, and wooden bridges lead to it on both sides. The river seldom rises and falls, but usually is the same depth in the winter as in the summer season, and it provides water which is very clear to the eye and very pleasant for one who wishes to drink . . . The winter too is rather mild there . . . And a good kind of vine grows thereabouts, and some persons have even managed to make fig-trees grow by covering them in winter.

Julian used Lutetia as a base to recuperate after his military campaigns, and lived on the Île de la Cité in an imperial palace that would later be home to the country's first kings. During his second winter in the city, in 360, Julian's own troops and the people of Lutetia proclaimed him Emperor Augustus, the highest rank possible. It was the first time the city had had such a prestigious inhabitant and protector, although it put him – and Lutetia – in direct conflict with Emperor Constantius II, ruler of the Romans' eastern territory. Julian was killed in battle in 363, and although further Roman leaders would use Lutetia as a base, it was, like the rest of Gaul and Europe, slowly slipping from their grip. Without a protector, Lutetia slipped behind the new regional capital of Sens in importance.

Shorn of its leaders and in constant danger of attack, Paris was seemingly in need of saints. Following the martyr Denis, several other individuals emerged who have left their mark on various districts of the city. St Martin became the subject of a cult after curing a leper by kissing him. St Marcel left an even greater trace – a village named after him that later became a district of Paris in recognition of his legendary ability to chase away monsters.

The inhabitants of a small community in today's 13th arrondissement were terrorized by a giant snake that lived in nearby marshland, and which had eaten a female sinner. The people, who were still mostly pagan, called on Marcel – a Parisian born and bred – for help. He came, found the snake, tapped it three times on the head with a cross and ordered it to slide away into the Seine. The beast, now docile, obeyed and was never seen again.

Perhaps the most significant of all the city's defenders, Geneviève, was born in about AD 422 in the suburb of Nanterre (where some believe the pre-Roman Lutetia lay). To her parents, she was something of a dreamer, and it was no surprise when she declared that she wanted to give up her life to God. Her parents were concerned, but later reassured by Germain, the bishop of Auxerre, who met Geneviève when he was passing through Nanterre and told them that he had seen 'something celestial' in the girl. Her parents – rich landowners of Gallo-Roman stock – died young but left her with a fortune. With the money, she moved to Paris, where she set up a convent school on the Île de la Cité. All of her money was spent on her faith, and she was known for the extreme frugality of her existence. She ate only two or three times a week, and then only a few beans and some bread. Since Paris was an important trade cross-roads, her reputation as a saintly individual spread across the world, but the practical, pragmatic Parisians were less impressed.

Although her legend was built largely on her piousness, it seems Geneviève was in fact a very capable diplomat. Her wealth enabled her to sit in on meetings of the city council, and to give her opinion on important matters in city life. It was at one of these meetings that the myth of Geneviève the saviour of the city began.

Word had arrived in Paris that Attila and the Huns were bearing down on the city. Attila had already attacked the western fringes of Gaul, and surely had an eye on the prize of Paris. The leaders of the city proposed a vote to abandon Paris in case of attack, but Geneviève argued that it should be defended at all costs. She also surprised the other members by announcing serenely that the Huns would not attack the city.

The men of Paris dismissed her opinion as superstitious nonsense, so Geneviève focused instead on winning over the women – their wives, mothers and daughters. She appealed to their sense of belonging: would it not break their hearts to abandon the place where they and their children were born?

One night in 451 the Huns were rumoured to be approaching the city gates. With mounting panic in the air, people began to pack their belongings and plan their exit. However, Geneviève and several of the women of the city locked themselves inside the church of Saint-Étienne on the Île de la Cité, scuppering the escape plan. Not wanting to leave without the women, the men returned home and waited. As Geneviève had predicted, the Huns began to move southwards, before being pushed back out of Gaul by an army of Romans and Visigoths.

After this victory, Geneviève's place in Parisian folklore was assured, and her myth would be resuscitated each time Paris was threatened. Her stock was high during her lifetime, too, and she chose to profit from this additional influence to construct a worthy temple to St Denis at the place where he had died.

In 476 the last Western Roman emperor, Romulus Augustus, abdicated, bringing the Roman Empire to an end and leaving a power vacuum across Europe. Paris was no longer a protected city, but a prize waiting to be claimed.

THE MAN WHO UNEARTHED LUTETIA

Théodore Vacquer, notes the historian Colin Jones, was a failed engineer and architect 'whose whole life was lived under the star of anonymity, isolation and non-achievement'. Despite this, during fifty years of stubborn and solitary digging, the nineteenth-century archaeologist managed to unearth just about everything we know about the Gallo-Roman settlement of Lutetia.

It has been said that if you want to know more about Lutetia, you can either get your hands dirty and sift through the soil of Paris, or delve into the 10,000 often enigmatic and indecipherable documents left behind by Vacquer, some of them little more than scribbled notes on the corners of restaurant tablecloths.

Vacquer's goal was to condense this material into the ultimate history of Paris, but to what must be the delight of procrastinators everywhere, he died before he produced anything. That is not to say that he did not leave behind a legacy, however. Despite being described by friends as 'a permanently rolled-up hedgehog', he was responsible for the creation of the archaeological collection in Paris's Musée Carnavalet, which opened in 1880.

The reluctance of Vacquer to share his discoveries is perhaps understandable. His digs shadowed the Haussmannian reconstruction of Paris, but the sites he was unearthing – small theatres, comfortable bourgeois homes – were simply not grand enough to fit the imperial vision of the new city. Paris was supposed to be as regal as Rome or Athens, not to have begun life as a provincial market town.

Vacquer's most crushing disappointment came at the Arènes de Lutèce. He uncovered the site during the digging of the new rue Monge, but his investigations were interrupted first by the Prussian invasion in 1870 and then by the city authorities allowing the Compagnie Générale des Omnibus to build a tram depot on the site. Much of the remains were swept away, leaving just the simulacrum of a Roman arena that we see today.

Nineteenth-century archaeological dig, possibly overseen by Théodore Vacquer, August 1873, rue de la Montagne.

The tombs of legendary lovers Pierre Abélard and Héloïse were transferred to the Père Lachaise cemetery in 1817.

2 The First Kings

As the last of the Roman rulers slunk away, an opening appeared for a new dynasty to assume control. First to take up the baton was the Salian Frank leader Childeric, who laid siege to Paris for ten years. During this period Geneviève performed another of her 'miracles' by sneaking out of the city on a moonless night and returning a few days later with a flotilla of boats loaded with wheat.

It was Childeric's son Clovis, though, who would build the reputation of the Merovingians, the first real French royal dynasty. Their arrival marked the passage from a Gallo-Roman to a Frankish community, but this was a reasonably painless process for Paris, possibly because most of the now-dominant Franks in the region were – as the historian Bruno Dumézil drolly states – 'simply Gallo-Romans transformed into barbarians in order to pay fewer taxes'. When Clovis inherited the throne from his father he was only fifteen, but already of age according to the law of the Franks (for whom majority came at the age of twelve). From the very beginning of his reign, Christianity played an important role. St Remigius, the bishop of Reims, wrote a letter to the young monarch he would later baptize, reminding him of the importance of the Church in Frankish society. 'Amuse yourself with young men, deliberate with the old', he advised, referring of course to the priests and bishops.

Clovis, however, was at first more interested in what would become a Merovingian characteristic: empire-building through warfare. A great warrior, he rapidly found significant success, claiming victories over remaining Gallo-Roman clans and other Frankish tribes in cities including Amiens, Soissons and Reims. Paris, at the heart of this territory, was the logical choice for his base, and he moved into the old Roman palace on the Île de la Cité, bringing a large court with him. From there he began to establish his dynasty by marrying off his family to leading members of other barbarian tribes – Visigoths and Burgundians – in order to create blood ties across the kingdom.

Once this largely unified kingdom was in place, Clovis turned to more spiritual matters. In about 496 he was baptized at Reims with around 3,000 of his troops, an event that cemented the alliance between the Frankish kingdom and the Roman Catholic Church. With the gusto and zeal of the born again, Clovis began covering Paris in churches and chapels. As with most previous developments in the city, the majority of these were on the Left Bank, but ecclesiastical construction also sparked off development on the Right. Clovis's conversion had possibly been organized by Paris's living saint, Geneviève, and the two formed close links. This proximity continued at the end of their lives: they died at roughly the same time, and were buried in the same place. Clovis died in 511, becoming the first 'Christian' king to be buried in Paris, probably alongside Geneviève in the crypt of the church of the Holy Apostles, the building they had planned together.

While Geneviève's tomb became a place of pilgrimage, and much later protest, Clovis's tomb has simply disappeared. Nevertheless, his influence lived on in many other ways. His (German) name was Latinized and then Gallicized into Louis, and eighteen French monarchs were subsequently given this title.

The church of the Holy Apostles, later renamed Abbaye Sainte-Geneviève de Paris, stood for 1,200 years before falling into decay. Louis xv ordered the building of a new church suitable for the city's patron saint, but construction was interrupted by the French Revolution. The building later became the secular temple that is the Panthéon today.

In a double affront in revolutionary Paris, in 1793 Geneviève's relics were also removed from the crypt and burned on the place de Grève (in front of the Hôtel de Ville). Today just an empty tomb is left in the church of Saint-Étienne-du-Mont alongside the Panthéon, but it remains an important place of pilgrimage, and Geneviève an enduring symbol of Paris.

After his death, the kingdom Clovis had built up was divided among his four sons. The northwestern segment – known as Neustria, and which included Brittany, Normandy and Paris – was inherited by Childebert. The four sons, living up to the Merovingian reputation as fantastically hirsute and violent rulers, organized the killing of their various nephews in order to ensure the succession of their own particular line. Only one of these young princes, Clodoald, managed to escape. The Merovingians were known for their long hair, and so Clodoald had been given an ultimatum: 'your hair or your life'. He gave up his Merovingian mane and became a hermit and monk – and was later known as St Cloud, giving his name to a wealthy western suburb of Paris.

In Paris, Childebert had returned from a Spanish adventure with the pilfered tunic of St Vincent. To house this valuable relic, he began building the basilica of Saint-Vincent-Saint-Croix, which would later become the abbey of Saint-Germain-des-Prés, one of the most powerful institutions in Paris. Continuing his father's church-building tendencies, Childebert also launched the building of the basilica of Saint-Étienne on the Île de la Cité, replacing a monument to Jupiter, roughly where Notre-Dame stands today. At 70 m (230 ft) long, it was the biggest church in the kingdom.

On 13 December 558 Childebert upstaged the solemn blessing of the new basilica by dying on the very day it was due to take place. Germain of Paris, the city's bishop, was a pragmatic man, though, and quickly organized a joint event – a blessing of the new building coupled with a royal funeral. At the end of the ceremony Childebert did not have far to go. He was buried in the crypt, a place he had already chosen for himself.

There remained only one son of Clovis, Clotaire, but he was already an old man and died three years later, again leaving a kingdom to be divided up between four sons. This time, Caribert was chosen for Paris, but he died very soon, presenting the three remaining brothers with something of a headache. Paris was clearly the most prestigious – and profitable – jewel in the crown, so which brother should take charge of it? Finally, they chose instead to carve up the tax income among them and establish a rule that no brother could enter the city without the permission of the other two. For the next seventeen years Paris existed without a clearly identified ruler.

These fraternal battles and inheritance problems continued until 629 and the death of Clotaire II, the last king to be buried in the abbey of Saint-Germain. He was succeeded by his son Dagobert, who renovated the church at Saint-Denis, transforming it into a true basilica. Dagobert himself was buried there, and thus began a royal association with Saint-Denis that lasted more than a thousand years.

The Merovingian dynasty came to an end in the middle of the eighth century when candidates for the throne simply ran out (not a surprise, given the enthusiasm with which they attacked one another's children). It was finally Pope Zachary who decided who should be king of the Franks, and he chose Pepin the Short, son of the famous warrior Charles Martel. The prestige of the new Carolingian dynasty was ensured when a pope (Stephen II), on a rare visit to the territory of the Franks, crowned and blessed Pepin at Saint-Denis.

The Carolingians were not good news for Paris. After being crowned king, Charlemagne, the son of Pepin and the first 'European' leader and a personality who is seen as equally important to French and German history, moved the court to Aachen in the east of his kingdom. Charlemagne – known also as Charles the Great – became the first Holy Roman Emperor, and his influence spread across most of Western Europe. Legend has it that he also created the first schools in France, despite being able neither to read nor write himself.

Paris returned to being a small port on the Seine, but it was still an important place in the eyes of its inhabitants.

Jean-Victor Schnetz, *Count Eudes Defending Paris against the Normans in 885*, 19th century. The first Châtelet tower can be seen in the background.

Abbo Cernuus, a monk and poet of the abbey of Saint-Germain-des-Prés, wrote that it was 'the city which, like a queen, shines brighter than all the others'. Indeed, so brightly did it shine that it soon attracted a new breed of invader from the north. Undefended and unprotected, Paris was an easy target for invaders, and in 845 the first Vikings arrived en masse to raid its riches. Abbo Cernuus was on hand to witness the repeated attacks, using just a little artistic licence to describe their scale. There were 'seven hundred sailing ships and other smaller craft, so numerous that it was impossible to count'. In fact, there were so many that it was impossible even to see the river: 'it wasn't visible any more; the wet pine, oak, elm and alder entirely covered its surface.'

The balance of forces was also in favour of the Vikings, according to Abbo: 'The courageous faithful numbered barely more than two hundred men, while the enemy numbered over forty thousand.' In charge of protecting the city was Eudes, the task given to him by the king 'not to cause the loss of the kingdom but rather to save it'. Despite being severely outnumbered (although not quite as severely as Abbo described), the Parisians held out, rebuilding protective towers overnight and making them nearly twice as big to surprise the invaders. They dusted down their faithful saints once again. They prayed at the tomb of St Germain and carried the relics of Ste Geneviève to the entrance to the city. Both saints came up trumps and helped to chase away the northern invaders. But, as Abbo admits, financial arguments were even more persuasive. To bring the first attack to a conclusion, Sigefroy, the king of the Vikings, accepted 60 livres 'of the purest silver'.

When King Charles III (the Fat) finally arrived in Paris during another Viking skirmish, he was 'surrounded by warriors from all the nations', but he still preferred to buy off the invaders with 700 livres rather than fight for the city. Charles's procrastination and cowardice brought discredit to the Carolingians. The various attacks, sieges and battles had strengthened the hand of Paris's defender Eudes, whom Abbo now happily labelled 'the greatest of princes since the beginning of this kingdom to this day'. Abbo, writing after the event, was being more than a little sycophantic, but it did demonstrate a sea change in the attitude of Parisians, who now looked more towards their count than to the king or the Holy Roman Emperor for guidance and leadership.

Eudes did indeed succeed Charles as king of the western Franks, and although the Carolingian dynasty returned after his death, his reign showed that power had moved to Paris and the Parisians, who were now positioned as the real king-makers. Decades of Viking vandalism on the Left Bank had left it in a piteous state, and subsequent rulers and city leaders began to build more and more on the Right Bank. These buildings of defence (the Grand Châtelet), religion and trade helped the Right Bank to assume a dominant role that it has never lost.

The Carolingian dynasty played itself out through the slapstick efforts of a procession of kings and princes (something of a feature of French royalty). Louis III forgot to duck when riding beneath a low doorframe, and his younger brother Carloman was killed by a wild boar while out hunting. Later Louis V reigned for only one year – becoming known in the

Middle Ages as 'the king who did nothing' – before he too succumbed to an equestrian/hunting episode aged only twenty. The dynasty died with him.

Hugh Capet, whose grandfather's brother had been Eudes, was elected to the throne in 987. He inherited a territory not much bigger than today's Paris region, but he still stamped *rex Francorum* – king of the Franks – on his coins and official papers.

For most historians, Capet's coronation marks the beginning of modern France, and this is because, after being largely forgotten or ignored by the Carolingians, Paris became the Capetian capital. The new dynasty was shaky at first, but the kings managed to keep it alive – and prevent counter-claims to the throne – by crowning offspring during their reign. Hugh Capet did this with his son Robert II, who succeeded him in 996. Robert was known as 'the Pious', despite being briefly excommunicated by the pope after he married his cousin Bertha. The marriage was annulled, and Robert remarried the Provençal schemer Constance of Arles. It was a loveless marriage, a fact that may not have been helped by Robert's regular insistence on inviting beggars and lepers into the royal palace on the Île de la Cité and publicly washing their feet.

Over the next century Paris slowly began to recover from its Viking-inflicted lacerations. The Right Bank continued its rapid development, profiting from a new port, through which supplies of meat and fish came into the city, as well as the gory and malodorous trades that went with the preparation of this produce. The city's Left Bank meanwhile stagnated and became sleepy, but it did accommodate the development of a teaching and learning infrastructure that was quickly acclaimed far beyond the French borders.

Part of this renown was down to such brilliant teachers as Pierre Abélard. In addition to being a gifted professor, Abélard has gone down in history as one of Paris's great lovers. After being something of a wandering student for many years, one of his first jobs was as tutor to the niece of a religious man in Paris, Canon Fulbert. The seventeen-year-old niece, Héloïse, quickly forgot her lessons in the arms of 38-year-old Abélard.

Market day in Saint-Denis.

THE CITY THAT LOST ITS HEAD

In his book *La Révolution de Paris* (2014), the writer and urbanist Paul-Hervé Lavessière traces a circular route around the edge of Paris, beginning and ending in Saint-Denis. Designed to be a new 130-km (81-mile) suburban *Grandes Randonnées* footpath, it has also been described by the book's publisher as the act of stitching the city's head back on to its body.

In addition to a circular path, this revolution refers to a key period for Saint-Denis. It was during the Terror, when the guillotine was at its busiest, that this area, fatally associated with royalty and spiritual superstition, was violently separated from the city. Since then Saint-Denis has forged a very different identity from Paris. Adopting the radical politics of the revolutionaries, it remains the only town in France of more than 100,000 inhabitants with a communist mayor. The town's attractive museum also chooses to highlight the revolutionary Paris Commune of 1871 rather than Saint-Denis' regal past, and even its most famous landmark is often overlooked. The basilica – burial place of the French royal family for a thousand years – became a cathedral in 1966, but not even the Métro system has taken this change of function into consideration.

This difference between the two municipalities can be seen three times a week, on Tuesday, Friday and Sunday, when the entire centre of Saint-Denis buzzes to the rhythm of the region's largest food market. Its three hundred stands, which spill across the main square and down the city's arteries, are a colourful reminder of the medieval Lendit Fair that, from the eleventh century, attracted traders from across Europe to the city each spring.

Since an estimated 36 per cent of its population was born outside France, Saint-Denis offers a vibrancy and diversity far in excess of anything to be found in Paris itself. The market, too, is an international bazaar, with products from southern Europe, Africa, the Antilles, and even the town itself. René Kersanté, Saint-Denis' last surviving market gardener, can often be found selling his lettuces, radishes, onions and courgettes at the market.

'The books were open,' Abélard recounted, 'but mixed in the lessons were more words of love than philosophy, more kisses than explanations.' The secret relationship produced a child, a fact that forced Abélard to marry Héloïse, although the couple, fearful that marriage would ruin his career in the Church, did not tell anyone about their union. Fulbert was furious with the stain on his family, and had Abélard castrated in the middle of the night. The distraught Héloïse chose to become a nun. The couple continued to send each other passionate letters, however. After spending time as a monk at Saint-Denis, Abélard returned to the city, where he became one of its most brilliant teachers and a founder of the University of Paris. The two lovers were eventually placed in the same tomb in Héloïse's convent, and then moved in the romantically inclined nineteenth century to the cemetery of Père Lachaise in the east of the city, where they lie under a heavy Gothic stone canopy.

Paris developed thanks to its growing trade links and learning establishments, but also because of the largesse of the Church. The city's religious institutions were important consumers of architecture, jewellery, glass and gold, and their financial support made Paris a centre of these industries. The combination of skilled craftsmen and large projects helped Gothic architecture to great importance in Paris, and Saint-Denis – and the first walls of Notre-Dame – were striking places of birth for the style.

Louis VII was behind the rebuilding of Saint-Denis and the plans for Notre-Dame, but he was not initially destined to be king. His elder brother, Prince Philippe, had already been chosen as the successor to their father, Louis VI, and crowned in Reims at the age of twelve. However, he became yet another royal victim of animals in 1131 when a wandering pig startled his horse, which threw him on to his head. Pigs were subsequently banned from the streets of Paris, and Louis, who had until then been destined for the Church, prepared to become king.

Louis VII became the first king to go on a crusade, and tellingly left Suger, abbot of Saint-Denis, in charge of the country during his two-year absence. The king later lost a wife – Eleanor of Aquitaine – to Henry Plantagenet of England, and then half a kingdom in subsequent battles. Fortunately, with his third wife he produced an heir who would prove one of France's greatest kings and one of the principal developers of Paris.

3 A City Defined

In the thirteenth century, like an ungainly teenager, Paris experienced a phenomenal growth spurt. Much of this sprouting was sparked by one of the city's greatest developers, Philippe II, who was later given the soubriquet 'Auguste', both to confer on him a more imperial edge and in reference to the month of his birth.

When Philippe ascended the throne, Paris had a population of 25,000; by the end of his reign it had doubled. A century later it was four times greater again, and the largest city in the Christian world. Philippe inherited the throne in 1180 aged fifteen, as had Clovis exactly seven hundred years before. Nicknamed *Dieudonné* (the god-given), he was the miraculous and no-longer-expected fruit of his hapless father's third marriage. The birth was even more crucial given that both an earlier wife of Philippe's father and his half-sister had married English Plantagenet princes.

The young Philippe was therefore nurtured, being crowned in Reims even before his father had died. Nevertheless, he had to count his lucky stars again to survive a severe fever he picked up after getting lost on a hunting trip. Once on the throne, though, the new king immediately demonstrated that he was not of a weak nature. In 1182 Philippe became the first ruler in a Christian country to expel the entire Jewish community. He implemented this extremely cynical policy not on questions of faith but instead to fill up the royal coffers. Those who refused to leave the country were put in prison, and set free only if they signed their wealth and property over to the king. Later Philippe would also cancel the totality of the debt owed to the Jewish community, but

Remains of the Philippe Auguste fortifications can still be found in many unusual places in the city, such as this example from rue Pavée in the Marais.

in return he obliged those who owed the money to repay one-fifth of the total to the Crown.

With the sums earned from this pillaging, Philippe set about transforming Paris. One of his first investments was the creation of a permanent market on the city's Right Bank – the original Les Halles structure – in a position where a market would stay for the next eight hundred years. For the first time, Paris boasted two covered stone buildings that enabled traders to keep their stock dry and fresh. These premium facilities and the associated creation of trading guilds made Paris a major commercial centre in Europe.

This neat organization of the city was a reflection of Philippe's obsession with cleanliness. Early in his reign he went one day to the window of his royal palace on the Île de la Cité to admire the Seine, but was instead thrown almost physically backwards by the foul smell of the street below. He declared that the city's streets should forthwith be paved, but very few were, and the muck and stench would remain a feature of Paris for hundreds of years.

The king's domestic tidying-up was interrupted when Pope Gregory VIII requested that Philippe and his English rival,

Richard I the Lionheart, forget their cross-Channel squabbles and set out together on a crusade to relieve Jerusalem from attack. Philippe accepted, but he knew that his absence would leave Paris vulnerable. Before leaving, he made a decision to protect his capital with a ring of massive stone walls and towers. Since it was assumed that the most likely threats would come from Normandy and England, construction was largely concentrated on the city's north-facing Right Bank. The imposing walls were 3 m (10 ft) thick, 20 m (66 ft) high, incorporated 33 towers and 24 gateways, and stretched for a little over 5 km (3 miles). At the westernmost edge of the wall was a colossal and austere fortress overlooking the Seine. This was the original Louvre.

The wall sent a powerful and defiant message to potential invaders. However, in addition to providing defence to Parisians, the fortifications were seen by the people of the city as a unifying element. For the first time since the Roman *oppidum* they were aware of being part of a clearly defined unit.

Despite Philippe's fears, the walls were never tested, and were eventually torn down and replaced by others further out. Although most sections were short-lived, the sheer mass ensured that chunks were incorporated into other buildings or simply left standing. Across today's city, many skeleton segments can still be seen poking out of courtyards or, more incongruously, in underground car parks.

Philippe's crusade was something of a disaster, and he arrived back in Paris on 4 July 1190 never having made it to Jerusalem, and with Richard the Lionheart once more a sworn enemy. Philippe managed to head off early conflict by arranging to have the English prince arrested and imprisoned, but that just made Richard even more determined to retaliate (although Richard would die before he had the opportunity).

The English and French spent the best part of the next twenty years skirmishing in northern France, although Paris always remained in Philippe's hands. The showdown came on 27 July 1214 at Bouvines near Lille – even if it was eventually played out without the English, whose army in France had disbanded a few months earlier. The battle – against one of the first significant European coalitions – is a key reference point in the conception of the French state, and victory cemented Philippe's reputation as one of the country's great leaders.

Philippe Auguste died in 1223, leaving Paris wealthy, solidly protected and firmly entrenched as the administrative centre of France. The only contemporary epitaph that is known of Philippe described him as 'a handsome, strapping fellow, bald but with a cheerful face of ruddy complexion, and a temperament much inclined towards good living, wine and women. He was generous to his friends, stingy towards those who displeased him, well versed in the art of stratagem, orthodox in belief, prudent and stubborn in his resolves. He made judgements with great speed and exactitude.' The French asked nothing more of their kings.

Philippe, like his father, had reigned for 43 years. His grandson Louis IX, rather curiously, reigned for the same period, and left his own mark on history, although not for entirely the same reasons. His father, Louis VIII, had sat on the throne for only three years, his most significant contribution to history his marriage to Blanche of Castile. The formidable Blanche acted as regent – Louis was only twelve years old when he was crowned – and retained a very strong influence on her son throughout her life.

Louis IX was marked by his extreme piety, and shortly after his death he became St Louis, the only canonized king of France. His dedication to the Catholic religion led him to spend a fortune on relics, and then another fortune on a building in which to house them. This grandiose display case was the suitably magnificent Sainte-Chapelle, constructed alongside the royal palace by the architect Pierre de Montreuil. Chief among the attractions was Christ's crown of thorns, which Louis bought from the emperor of Constantinople for six times the sum that he had spent on building the Sainte-Chapelle itself.

In addition to promoting the glory of the Church, Louis was keen to encourage learning in Paris. In the middle of the thirteenth century (1257) an institution was created that remains one of the most recognized names of Paris today:

the Sorbonne. It took its name from its founder, Robert de Sorbon, a scholar and theologian who helped to raise the renown of the college above many other competing establishments through his charisma and the quality of his teaching. Such institutions firmly established Paris as one of Europe's most important centres of learning, attracting more than 10,000 scholars from across the continent. Life for students in the city, though, was mostly a terrible one, the sheer concentration of numbers in a relatively small area bringing noise, debauchery, lewdness and much brawling.

Typically such students lived 'in a poor house with an old woman who cooks only vegetables and never prepares a sheep except on feast days . . . After the meal, a student sits on a rickety chair and uses a light, doubtless a candle, which goes out continuously and disturbs the ideas.' The students paid a small fortune for this privilege, and then had to find additional money to pay their master. Lessons began at 5 am and were often held – in all weathers – on straw bales in the street. Despite their hunger and tiredness, students who were slow to grasp a lesson would quickly feel their master's stick. Nevertheless, education, along with the Church, offered young people a way to progress in society.

With his devout nature, Louis was easily tempted away from Paris on crusades, but these exotic adventures brought him little luck. On his first crusade he was captured in Egypt and freed only after a large ransom was paid. He returned to Paris to discover that his mother had died during his absence. On his second crusade, this time in Tunisia, an attack of dysentery brought his own life to an end.

After a good run of successful and generally well-liked kings, it was perhaps inevitable that a pantomime villain should eventually take up residence in Paris. This role would be played by Philippe IV (the Fair), whose reign began in 1285. His list of faults was a long one, and included being a spendthrift, a bigot, a liar, a usurper and a thoroughly violent man.

Philippe began by emptying the royal coffers to pay for the embellishment of the royal palace on the Île de la Cité, although this did at least bring together all the major

Pierre de Montreuil's masterpiece, the Sainte-Chapelle.

institutions under one roof. To cover the excess cost of the project the king invented new taxes, but when this led to rioting, he moved on to the pockets of the Jewish community.

Not wanting to share any power or influence in his kingdom, Philippe set about attacking his two main rivals: the pope and the Knights Templar. Philippe's forces chased the pope to exhaustion in Italy, and then installed a French puppet pontiff (Clement v) in the post, which Philippe decreed should now be based in the French city of Avignon.

The Templars were the unofficial treasurers and bankers of the nation. Installed in the Temple – an almost entirely independent city on the edge of Paris – they saw themselves as answering directly to the pope rather than to a French king. But with Clement v in place, that independent protection disappeared. On Friday 13 October 1307 Philippe sent his army into the Temple and had all the Templars arrested on trumped-up charges that included corruption, heresy and the promotion of homosexuality. Some 138 people were quickly burned at the stake, but the final trial of the leaders did not take place until 1314. During the trial, which was held in front

Meeting of doctors at the University of Paris; miniature from the *Chants Royaux* manuscript, 16th century.

of Notre-Dame, they were given two options: life imprisonment if they accepted their guilt, or immediate burning at the stake if they continued to proclaim their innocence. The men chose the second option.

According to Geoffroy de Paris, a chronicler who witnessed the event, the principal leader, Jacques de Molay, cried out a curse just before his death: 'God knows who is in the wrong and who has sinned. Soon misfortune will come upon those who have unjustly condemned us. God will avenge our death.' Pope Clement died 42 days later (although he had apparently been ill for some time), but, more unexpectedly, Philippe the Fair died eight months later after a fall from a horse. Fourteen years later the direct line of the Capetian dynasty came to an end after the premature deaths of both of Philippe's sons before they had managed to produce an heir.

De Molay had perhaps been avenged, but he had also inadvertently provoked a constitutional crisis that would plunge France into a long and disastrous war. As the grandson of Philippe, the successor to the throne should probably have been Edward III of England, but his claim was through a female line – and from an unfriendly neighbour. In 1337 the French nobility instead chose Philippe VI de Valois, sparking the Hundred Years War – a conflict that would famously last 114 years.

The fourteenth century was a terrible time for Paris, with poor harvests, peasant uprisings, civil war and disease. In 1348 about eight hundred people a day were dying of the Black Death. Such misery and desperation led to an increase in crime, and in consequence ever more vicious punishments. The city's dreaded Montfaucon gibbet, a wooden execution post, was replaced by a 10-m- (33-ft-) high solid stone version that could hold dozens of victims on three levels. The hanging bodies were left to rot – and stink – for weeks, in full view of Parisians, before slowly being devoured by crows.

In 1356 Philippe's successor, Jean the Good, was captured by the English at the Battle of Poitiers and taken to England. His son, the future Charles V, was left behind to cobble together the crippling sums demanded as a ransom (an agreement that also included handing over a third of the country). When Charles came knocking on the door of Paris, Étienne Marcel, provost of the city's merchants, spotted an opportunity to demand administrative reform and greater

NOTRE-DAME DE PARIS

In a letter sent shortly after the publication of Victor Hugo's *Notre-Dame de Paris* (1831; published in English as *The Hunchback of Notre-Dame*), Honoré de Balzac described the novel as 'implausible' and 'a deluge of bad taste'. When composing his rather snooty dispatch, little did Balzac imagine that this 'boring' book would not only remain a cultural staple for nearly two centuries, but would affect the way Paris appears today.

The myth created by the novel has been so powerful that it can be difficult to separate the book from the building. This duality was immediately noted by Jules Michelet, a historian and contemporary of Hugo, who wrote, 'He has built, alongside the old cathedral, a cathedral of poetry, as solid as the foundations of the other, as high as its towers.'

Hugo's Notre-Dame dates from 1482, a gloomy but magnificent haunted castle borrowed from the genre of the gothic novel. Although he claimed the book had 'no historical pretensions', he lovingly created an accurate picture of fifteenth-century Paris, complete with the dreaded three-storey Montfaucon gibbet and the rotten but joyous Cour des Miracles slums.

Visitors to the cathedral today may imagine that they are seeing that fifteenth-century building, but what they are actually observing is a reflection of Hugo's vision. Victor Hugo was very active in early preservation movements in Paris, and was particularly scathing towards the renovators who he believed favoured industry over art.

Hugo's historical opus became a powerful war machine in the city's heritage battle, and was instantly influential. One of his chief targets was the Neoclassical architect Étienne-Hippolyte Godde, who had been suggested for a post-Revolution renovation job on Notre-Dame. With Hugo's novel in mind and the vogue for all things medieval, the commission eventually went to Eugène Viollet-le-Duc and Jean-Baptiste Lassus, who completed the neo-Gothic makeover we see today.

The city's Catholic leaders never liked Hugo's book, believing it to be irreligious and immoral, but the Church can nevertheless be thankful for one thing: that by being stronger than Godde, Hugo ensured that Paris's principal divine building became the city's most visited monument.

The Notre-Dame cathedral is almost inseparable from Victor Hugo's tale, here depicted by François Chifflart in an 1831 edition of *Notre-Dame de Paris*.

power for the people. Charles had no choice but to accept, especially after Marcel organized the killing of two of his advisers under his nose. The prince regent, however, swiftly escaped and would soon return in triumph. Marcel himself was killed in Paris by his own supporters, who turned against him after he made a number of perceived bad alliances.

Charles v became king in 1364, shortly after Edward iii had renounced his own claim to the French throne. Charles, a great builder, created a new set of city walls on the Right Bank, including the imposing fortress of the Bastille. Not a single element of these walls is left today, but they influenced future development in the city, notably the Grands Boulevards between Bastille and Opéra.

Remembering the affront he had suffered at the hands of Marcel in the palace on the Île de la Cité, Charles moved the royal family out of Paris altogether. They lodged at the newly constructed Hôtel Saint-Pol just outside the city walls, a turreted palace that was protected both by the neighbouring Bastille and by the lions Charles kept in the gardens. Charles also redeveloped the royal castle at Vincennes, where he had been born, adding an immense donjon tower and fortified walls. In Paris itself, Charles transformed the old fortress of the Louvre into a more regal medieval palace, adding windows, turrets and a royal library. Somewhat bizarrely, the underground remnants of this particular incarnation of the Louvre are today visible from a McDonald's outlet in the Carrousel du Louvre shopping centre.

Paris was growing, but it was still suffering. The new monarch Charles vi started as the 'Bien Aimé' (beloved), before slowly coming to be known as 'le Fol' (the mad) when frequent bouts of psychosis altered his behaviour (he believed he was made of glass and would do all he could to avoid being smashed). Such leadership did not help a country at war, and in 1415 the French suffered a terrible defeat at Agincourt.

After Agincourt, the English took over the city of Rouen before approaching Paris. With the help of their allies the Normans and the Burgundians, Paris was run for fifteen years by an Englishman, the Duke of Bedford. In 1429 Joan of Arc led a small army towards Paris with the goal of liberating the city, but could not force her way in and was injured at the porte Saint-Honoré. She was eventually captured by the Burgundians, tried by the Church and burned at the stake in Rouen.

Now that a peace accord with the English had finally been signed, the French kings settled down to a life of leisure in the chateaux of the Loire valley (Chambord, Amboise), far from the urban plotting and intrigue of Paris. The only dangers they suffered in this bucolic and languid environment were of their own making. Charles VIII, for example, brought his own reign to an end at the age of 28 after forgetting to duck when walking through a low doorway in Amboise.

One man who was constantly in danger of hitting his head on doorways was François I, who became king in 1515. He was nearly 2 m (6 1/2 ft) tall and 'every inch the Renaissance king'. Obsessed with Italy and its culture, he brought many artists to France, including Leonardo da Vinci, who later died in his arms. Although Paris missed much of the Renaissance, François did commission the architects Pierre Lescot and Jean Goujon to rebuild the Louvre to house his art collection. As well as fostering art and architecture, François founded the Collège de France and imposed French as the exclusive and obligatory language of the state – a decree that is still in force today. A constantly active ruler, he died in 1547, worn out, as the historian Alistair Horne puts it, 'by war, hunting and sex'. His immense tomb in Saint-Denis is a monument to the size and importance of this singular king.

The monarchy returned to Paris with Henri II who, significantly, had married Catherine de Medici, a niece of the pope. It took a decade for the couple to produce an heir, but they eventually had ten children, three of whom became kings. Continuing a long line of avoidable and ridiculous royal deaths, Henri was killed in a jousting accident at a tournament that had been organized in the palace at Tournelles as part of the wedding celebrations of two of his children. Following the accident, Catherine ordered the destruction of one of the Marais' most magnificent palaces.

The St Bartholomew's Day Massacre saw a frenzy of killing on the streets of Paris. Painting by François Dubois, *c.* 1572–84, oil on panel.

After the young François II died, just a few months into his reign, the crown was passed on to his brother Charles IX, who was only ten years old. Catherine became regent, but was the effective ruler of the country, even after Charles had come of age. A staunchly Catholic Italian, she became embroiled in the wars of religion that had broken out across France.

With the new Protestantism gaining influence across Europe, thanks to the writings of Martin Luther and Jean Calvin, the French royal family began giving tacit approval to attacks on the reformists. On 24 August 1572 the most terrible attack of all took place in Paris, although the events leading up to this massacre had originally brought hope of reconciliation between Catholics and Protestants.

Catherine had organized the wedding of her daughter – the king's sister – Margot to a Protestant prince, Henri of Navarre. The wedding took place in Paris on 18 August, and was followed by several days of feasting, before the party came to an abrupt end. Religious tension was still high, particularly in the rabidly Catholic French capital, and the arrival of thousands of Protestants for the festivities did not sit well. For an undetermined reason, the city gates were shut and the ringing of bells in the church of Saint-Germain

l'Auxerrois early in the morning of 24 August signalled
the beginning of crazed attacks by Catholics of the city on
the Protestant population in Paris. During this so-called St
Bartholomew's Day Massacre, some 15,000 Protestants were
killed. Henri of Navarre, who would later become king, was
spared after he promised to convert to Catholicism.

Barely two years after the massacre, Charles ix died at
the Vincennes chateau, ostensibly of an illness (pleurisy)
allegedly exacerbated by guilt. Rumours also circulated that
a poison administered by his mother helped to hasten his
demise. His death left the throne vacant for the third son
of Henri ii and Catherine, Henri iii. Possibly homosexual
and certainly flamboyant, Henri was known for surrounding
himself with *mignons* – his court favourites – and for dressing
in the latest fashion. Such extravagance made him deeply
unpopular, but it was the fact that he had no children – and
apparently no intention of producing any – that made him
dangerous for many.

Henri iii declared that Henri of Navarre (his cousin twenty
times removed, and a survivor of the massacre), still very much
a Protestant, should be his heir, causing consternation across
the country. The critical moment of this passage of power was
brought forward in 1589 when a fanatical monk named Jacques
Clément plunged a knife into the king's stomach as he stood
up from the toilet. 'Méchant! Tu m'as tué!' (Villain! You've
killed me!) cried Henri, his breeches still around his ankles.

The king was dead. Paris would not see a new one for the
next five years.

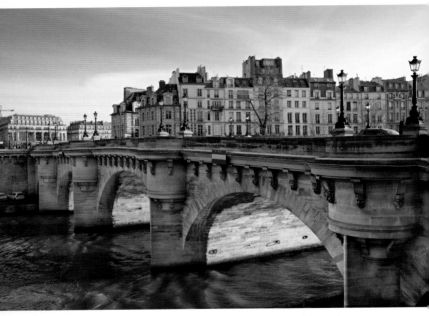

The pont Neuf and the entrance to the place Dauphine, two of the major developments completed during the reign of Henri IV.

4 The First Modern City

Paris ended the sixteenth century in dispute and duplicity, but began the seventeenth – in many ways the city's defining era – in a much better frame of mind. The man who would help to make that change was Henri iv, but in 1589, after the assassination of Henri iii, his installation in Paris was anything but certain. With the wounds of the Wars of Religion still raw in France, the idea of a Protestant ruler was an impossibility for many, particularly in Paris, which had grown used to being a kingless city. The French capital – controlled by the extremist Catholic League – was put under siege for five years, causing immeasurable suffering. Perhaps because of severe war-weariness, perhaps because of Henri's rather cynical conversion to Catholicism at Saint-Denis in 1593 ('Paris vaut bien une masse' [Paris is worth a Mass], he is famously alleged to have declared), the city was finally ready to welcome its new ruler in March 1594. Henri chose to arrive in Paris very early in the morning, although he need not have been so cautious. There were no cheering crowds, but neither were there barriers or resistance. What he found was a city in a terrible state, medieval in form and function, with the crumbling Île de la Cité still at its heart.

Finally gaining power in his early forties, Henri was keen to make up for lost time. He showed remarkable energy, earning himself the nickname 'Vert Galant' (an affectionate phrase somewhat akin to 'old bandit'). In addition to his passion for building and renovation, he had a typical Bourbon thirst for sex. Legend has it that during his life he entertained 73 mistresses and fathered 22 children. His energy was welcome, since Paris was literally falling apart. On 22 December 1596 the pont aux

Meuniers, a medieval bridge typically overloaded with houses, toppled into the Seine, killing 150 people. Fortunately for the city, a new kind of bridge was already under construction, although it was much delayed by war and siege. Henri pushed for rapid completion of this 'pont Neuf' ('new bridge', but now the city's oldest), partly by instigating a novel way to ensure its funding. He placed a tax on all casks of wine entering the city, prompting Henri Sauval, a Paris historian writing in the 1660s, to note that the bridge was paid for by 'the rich and drunkards'.

Built solidly in stone, the pont Neuf was also extremely functional, since its 270-m (886-ft) span finally opened up direct access between the city's Left and Right banks. In addition to its practical role, its reputation was quickly established as a place of pleasure, leisure and commerce. The bridge boasted some of the city's first proper pavements and a series of alcoves, like theatre balconies, that offered wonderful views of the river, the Île de la Cité and the Louvre. The pont Neuf rapidly became one of the most populated parts of the city and, as the Parisian proverb had it, there was 'not a moment of the day on which one did not see a carriage, a white horse, a priest and a prostitute'.

Henri IV finally arrives in Paris: François Gérard, *Entrée d'Henri IV à Paris, 22 mars 1594*, 1817, oil on canvas.

Henri announced, through the voice of his provost marshal, that he intended to 'spend years in this city, and live there like a true patriot, to make this city beautiful, tranquil, and full of the conveniences that will be possible'. Most of all, though, he wanted to 'make a whole world of this city and a wonder of the world'. It was no sooner said than done. 'As soon as he was master of Paris,' declared one witness, 'you could see construction workers all over the city.'

Desiring a solid, harmonious city, Henri was the first person to introduce planning regulations in Paris, notably banning the use of wood in favour of local stone and brick. The perfect example was the place Royale, today's place des Vosges. The square was originally an extension of a silk works the king had tried to install to encourage the creation of wealth in Paris, but it soon became one of the most fashionable addresses in the city. It had three main goals: to adorn Paris, to provide a setting for public ceremony and to offer a recreational space for Parisians. This was a radically new idea, not just for Paris but for Europe as a whole. The square was literally a square (rather than the much larger rectangles seen elsewhere across the Continent), and was built with no religious or political function in mind, and no single stand-out building. It was simply a celebration of its own beauty, its covered walkways and vibrant red-brick mansions 'on a scale', points out the historian Joan DeJean, 'that until then had been reserved for royal palaces'.

Henri's other major construction was the place Dauphine, a speculative project on land that had belonged to the royal palace on the Île de la Cité. Situated halfway across the pont Neuf and begun in 1607, the development profited from the immense popularity of the bridge. It was a great success and changed the living habits of the Parisian bourgeoisie, who were soon congregating in such dedicated spaces in the city.

Henri iv did much to make Paris an attractive and bustling city, but he himself became a victim of the traffic jams this caused. Travelling through the centre of Paris, his carriage was blocked in rue de la Ferronnerie (near the city's principal market), giving François Ravaillac – a failed monk

The place des Vosges: some of the most exclusive terraced housing in the world.

and teacher, as well as a fanatical Catholic – time to jump up on to the plate and stab Henri, using a kitchen knife he had stolen from a nearby inn. Henri became the second king in succession to be assassinated, but unlike the previous Henri, the death of the 'Vert Galent' helped to forge his myth. His apparently special powers continued to fascinate his subjects long after his death. When all the royal tombs were opened in Saint-Denis during the French Revolution, Henri's body was said to be still recognizable, and sporting such a handsome white beard that a soldier treacherously cut off a few whiskers as a lucky charm.

Henri was succeeded by eight-year-old Louis XIII, the first of three child kings in a row – an unusual and potentially dangerous situation for France. Louis's mother, Marie de Medici, ruled as regent, but the reign was eventually given lasting significance by Cardinal Richelieu, the king's principal minister.

In his early life, Louis spent most of his time in his mother's Luxembourg palace, chasing hares and boar in the vast gardens. The polar opposite of his boisterous father, he was said to be timid and morose. He had little interest in women – possibly more interest in men – and that was not helped by his early

Henri IV on horseback surveys the place Dauphine.

forced engagement to Anne of Austria. It would take more than twenty years to produce an heir, the future Louis XIV, a child who immediately became known as the 'enfant du miracle' (miracle child). Most of Louis XIII's reign was played out in the shadow of the Europe-wide Thirty Years War, but the king was largely absent from that, as he was from many other important matters of state, preferring the sport in his royal forests. Instead, he listened to whatever Richelieu suggested.

Despite such royal lethargy, Paris continued to develop, and several important new buildings were constructed, notably Richelieu's home, the Palais-Royal. The triumph, though, was the Île Saint-Louis, a unique structure and a marvel of technology and innovation. The development joined two small islands, and construction was for the first time plotted in a grid. The streets were about 60 per cent wider than those elsewhere in Paris, and have been left largely untouched since they were laid down. The final touches were the extraordinary private homes, particularly Louis Le Vau's Hôtel Lambert, which ensured early occupation of the island by the city's bourgeoisie. The buildings also seemed to go up remarkably quickly: 'I thought this morning I'd seen an enchanted island:

The Institut de France, home to the Académie française since 1795.

THE FRENCH DEFENDERS

> The primary function of the Académie will be to work, with all care and diligence possible, to give definite rules to our language and to render it pure, eloquent and capable of dealing with the arts and sciences.

When the Académie française was created in 1634 by Cardinal Richelieu, Louis XIII's chief minister, article 24 of its charter made the Académie's mission very clear: to bring order and nobility to an anarchic language that was not spoken – or worse, was spoken extremely badly – by more than half of the population of the country.

It was François I who had first decided, a hundred years earlier, that French should be used for all official documents, but since that decree, the French language had struggled to replicate the regal glory of Latin. For a nation of semi-independent states, each with its own language or dialect, French would be the thread that would stitch the country together.

The main tool of the Académie is its official dictionary, although only eight editions have been published since its creation. The ninth was begun in the 1980s; today the forty *immortels* (its members, who have a chair for life once voted in, unless – like Marshal Pétain – they are removed for 'misconduct') are still discussing words beginning with the letter 'R'.

Although the Académie undoubtedly helped to establish the French language as one of the purest in the world, it has more recently become a victim of its own eccentricities. This is not because of the slightly absurd *habit vert* its members are obliged to wear (a costume that also includes a sword, but not for members of the clergy, or for women – the first of whom became a member in 1980), but rather the ever-increasing average age of the *académiciens*. As the writer Georges Bernanos put it rather succinctly, 'when I've only got my arse left to think with, then I'll go and sit on the Académie française.'

I left it deserted, and I found it inhabited,' quipped the poet Pierre Corneille.

Richelieu and Louis died within six months of each other in 1642 and 1643, with Louis sharing his date of death with his father (14 May). Louis was only 41 years old when he died, which meant another premature passage of power, this time to the dauphin – Louis XIV – who was only three. He would eventually prove to be the country's most flamboyant and extravagant ruler – the 'Roi Soleil', or Sun King – propelling France to the top of the world (while also allowing it to career dangerously towards financial ruin), but the beginning of his reign was not auspicious. Since he was so young, his mother, Anne of Austria, ruled at first, aided by Richelieu's successor, the Italian Giulio Mazzarini, better known as Cardinal Jules Mazarin. Mazarin would never be popular with Parisians, partly because it was said that he never learned to speak French properly.

With the Thirty Years War drawing to a close, France was nearly bankrupt. In a desperate search for revenue, Mazarin and Anne decided to raise taxes, an act that inevitably provoked

Hôtel Lambert on the Île Saint-Louis.

uproar in parliament. Keen to demonstrate that the Crown – although a regency – was not weak, Anne organized the arrest of the leader of parliament, Pierre Broussel. Almost immediately, some 100,000 Parisians built barricades in the streets and took up arms against royal forces.

This action marked the beginning of the Fronde, a series of civil wars named after a stone-flinging catapult used by children. Living in the thinly defended Palais-Royal rather than the more fortress-like Louvre, Anne decided to whisk the infant Louis away to the relative safety of the royal palace in Saint-Germain-en-Laye, to the west of Paris. The entire royal court – which had begun to enjoy itself in the festive Palais-Royal – was forced to follow. From a life of luxury and indulgence, they found themselves sleeping on the cold floor of a medieval chateau that was unprepared for their arrival.

In an attempt to tame the rebellious city quickly, Anne sent a dashing general, the Prince of Condé, to lay siege to Paris. The blockade began just as a bitterly cold winter was hitting hardest, and food shortages were rapidly felt by the population. The queen regent's actions were efficient, but they also led to increased opposition, in particular to Mazarin. Nevertheless, a peace treaty was signed that enabled the court to return to the city.

In 1652, however, Louis was forced to leave Paris again when a second conflict, the Fronde des Princes, broke out. Violent conflict spread across Paris and it was often difficult to ascertain who was fighting whom. The Prince of Condé had switched sides and was nearly slaughtered, saved only by Mademoiselle de Montpensier (who was known afterwards as La Grande Mademoiselle) firing on the opposing army from a cannon on top of the Bastille tower. This mademoiselle had been a potential match for Louis, but spoiled her chances by firing the cannon in his direction. She had 'killed her husband', Mazarin later declared.

The Fronde burned itself out after a city mob set fire to the Hôtel de Ville, killing more than a hundred people. Tired of years of infighting and chaos, Parisians requested the return of the king, who eventually came back to the city

– now at an age to rule – on 21 October 1652. Unwittingly, and certainly counterproductively, the Fronde had paved the way for an absolutist monarchy. The king's new-found popularity was demonstrated spectacularly in 1660 after his marriage to Maria Theresa of Spain. Louis organized a grand promenade through Paris, with 100,000 people – one-quarter of the population of the city – waving the couple on its way. The well-wishers included Jean de La Fontaine and Jean Racine, both of whom composed odes to this 'roi qui de son nom remplit tout l'univers'. As the historian Alistair Horne pointed out, though, 'they would never be that close to him again, or indeed any other French monarch.'

For Louis, the turning point was the death of Mazarin in 1661. Left without his second father, the king set up home in the more easily defendable Louvre and decided to rule alone. His famous declaration 'L'état c'est moi' was now an undisputed reality. After assuming full powers, the king set to work on building his myth. In 1662 the royal couple organized a grand party to celebrate the birth of an heir. Obsessed, as most French rulers were, with Rome, Louis dressed as an emperor, a splendid sun prominent on his shield. Thus was born the legend of the Sun King.

Louis had good reason to be satisfied. He was a radiant and youthful king in the most dynamic country in Europe. France was by this time the most populous country on the Continent – with more than three times the population of England – and Paris easily the biggest city. Nevertheless, Louis, who had never forgiven nor forgotten the *frondeurs*, had fallen out of love with his capital, and decided to move the court to somewhere more suitably regal. This would involve a vast rebuilding of the Crown's chateau in Versailles, inspired by a building to the southeast of Paris, Vaux le Vicomte (by the same architect – Le Vau – and landscaper – André Le Nôtre), the over-extravagant home of Nicolas Fouquet. For his cheek in daring to build a house more regal than the king's, Fouquet was arrested by the Comte d'Artagnan, later fictionalized in Alexandre Dumas' novel *The Three Musketeers*.

Louis XIV puts his best foot forward in Versailles.

Versailles was not only a temple to megalomania, but a vast complex that had to house the entire court and the country's nobility where Louis could keep an eye on them. It was home to anywhere between two and five thousand people, often in very basic accommodation (when they could have been enjoying their own spacious country estates). This also had the effect of creating a generation of absentee landlords, which would later prove extremely dangerous for the country.

Between 1670 and 1714 Louis returned to Paris only 25 times, but the city nevertheless managed to flourish. Major building programmes in this period included the embellishment of the Champs-Élysées, Les Invalides military hospital, the church of Saint-Sulpice, the delicate and modest place des Victoires (albeit with a bombastic statue of Louis at its centre) and the decidedly less modest place Vendôme. Everything built in the city was required to reflect the glory of Louis XIV, but it also inspired a golden age of architects, with Le Vau, Libéral Bruant and Jules Hardouin-Mansart all adding masterpieces to the city's skyline.

The major revolution in Paris, however, was its transformation into an open city. After the Vauban defences – believed to be unbreakable – were erected at the perimeter of the country, Louis declared that Paris no longer needed city walls. The old Charles V fortifications were therefore torn down and replaced with a 'boulevard', a tree-lined walkway ringing the city. It was a remarkable and unique situation in Europe, which reflected not only the confidence of Louis, but also his desire to make Paris a less enclosed society – and to cause Parisians to feel slightly less secure.

During Louis' reign, France grew rich. The Crown's income went from 18 million livres in 1590 to 109 million in 1653. The king's revenue was four times greater than that of the English king, but all the money was quickly spent, mostly on the running of the royal court and on warfare. Funds came primarily from financial speculation, but also through France's new role as the fashion leader of Europe, with Paris at its centre. This suited all parties, as the historian Joan DeJean points out: 'Luxury goods became an industry for France because all involved, seventeenth-century merchants as much as their monarch, recognized the added value of promoting the dream of Paris and the reputation of its stylish inhabitants.'

These fashions were developed and promoted by the younger generation of nobles who had started to return to Paris, but among the older generation at court, boredom began to set in as Versailles became more akin to a retirement home. An era based on pleasure and leisure was transformed into an age of sobriety, notably after Madame de Maintenon, Louis' final mistress, took control and began her 'long struggle for the King's soul'. The ageing and steadily more morose Louis accepted that this struggle would be a difficult task. 'God seems to have forgotten all I have done for him,' he complained, after defeat in another of his ever more ruinous and largely pointless battles. Later, on his deathbed, he recognized that his taste for conflict and spending had hurt the country. 'Try to be at peace with your neighbours. I have loved war too much. Do not imitate me in that, nor in my too great expenditure,' he advised his young heir.

As if mirroring the dying of an era, the winter of 1709–10 was one of the coldest ever in Paris. More than 20,000 Parisians died of cold, including the king's confessor, François d'Aix de La Chaise, better known to posterity as Père Lachaise. Louis was 71 years old; he had reigned for more than 65 years, and the question of succession became more and more pressing – even more so following the premature deaths of most of his offspring.

Louis had fathered six legitimate children, but by 1709 five had died (mostly of smallpox or measles), leaving just the Grand Dauphin – who died himself in 1711. Two of the king's grandchildren also died, in 1712 and 1714, and a third, Philippe, Duke of Anjou, had become king of Spain and was therefore forbidden from taking the French crown. There remained a great-grandchild, another Louis, who would shortly become Louis xv.

Louis xiv died in 1715 after 72 years on the throne, the longest reign in France's history. Between 1615 and 1715 France had been at war with foreign enemies for a total of sixty years, and had suffered civil war for an additional five years. The country was in need of a period of peaceful austerity. But since Louis xv was just five years old, it was his dashing cousin (who was also his great-uncle), Philippe, Duke of Orléans, who took over as regent, and austerity was not really his thing. His first act was to bring the court back to Paris, which was far more to his rakish tastes than Versailles, and the Palais-Royal became the centre of France once again.

The regency marked a renaissance for the city, and the religious sobriety of Madame de Maintenon was quickly forgotten by the nobility. Paris instead sparkled with cafés, spectacles and salons. 'All the pleasures and all the delights of life are, in Paris, so near to the hands of those who can take them that you must be of a very indifferent nature not to abuse the possibility of tasting them,' explained the playwright Marivaux in his *Lettres sur les habitants de Paris* of 1717–18. Indeed, such temptations were everywhere, with shops being 'cut-throat for the good people who do not have the strength to say no'.

If Paris were not restrained and sober, the king certainly was. Described as frail, gloomy and cold, he wasted no time in whisking the court back to Versailles when his uncle died in 1723. Then aged thirteen, Louis took control of the country with the help of another uncle, the Duke of Bourbon, but this time most of the nobility chose not to follow him, and the monarch became dangerously isolated. Two years later Louis married the daughter of an exiled king of Poland, and although the couple barely spoke, the marriage still produced ten children in ten years. Rather than take council from his wife, Louis allowed the country to be run by his two mistresses; first Madame de Pompadour, for two decades, and then the much-hated Madame du Barry.

Madame de Pompadour was at least a patron of Paris, encouraging artists and the Enlightenment movement and helping to execute a number of important architectural projects in the city. She was instrumental in the development of the place de la Concorde – known at the time as the place Louis xv – and the vast École Militaire, both designed by Ange-Jacques Gabriel.

'Paris is crawling with beautiful minds: there have never been so many,' wrote Marivaux, who could count himself among that number. If, as he remarked, 'a little like in an army, there are few General Officers, many Junior Officers and an infinite number of soldiers', the city could nonetheless consider itself to be in a golden age of art and philosophy, with Voltaire, Rousseau and Diderot at the head of the troops.

On the real military front, France had slipped back into expensive bad habits. The country had become embroiled in the Seven Years War on several continents, and the concluding Peace of Paris of 1763 represented a significant defeat. France lost its nascent empire in Canada, India and the United States to the British, as well as its position as the dominant European nation – and French as the dominant language. Two years later France expanded with the acquisition (from the Republic of Genoa) of Corsica, from where one of the country's most significant rulers would shortly emerge.

Known as Louis 'le Bien-Aimé' (the Beloved) when producing numerous offspring and presiding over a stable country, the king had by the end of his long reign – 59 years – been transformed by military defeat and political instability into 'le Mal-Aimé' (the Unloved). He died in May 1774 of smallpox, alone, after the court was sent away to avoid infection, and his burial was carried out secretly at night in Saint-Denis, witnessed by just a few brave souls. His grandson, yet another Louis, inherited the throne at the age of twenty. With an adult on the throne at last after more than 150 years of reigns beginning shakily with children and regencies, there was genuine hope that a more modern and egalitarian form of monarchy would emerge. But those hopes were soon dashed, as France hurtled ever faster towards internal conflict.

5 Revolution and Restoration

That things would not work out well for Louis XVI and Marie Antoinette could have been guessed from their marriage celebrations. On 16 May 1770 the bride and groom – she fourteen years of age, he just a year older – were married at Versailles, initiating a partnership that had little to do with love and everything to do with politics. Marie Antoinette was the second youngest of sixteen children. Her father was Francis I, the Holy Roman Emperor and ruler of Austria, a country that had been an enemy of France but was now a fragile ally. To cement the shaky relations, a swift Habsburg–Bourbon alliance by marriage was deemed essential.

The festivities at Versailles were largely spoiled by storms, but it was the celebrations in Paris that would signal dark clouds ahead for the couple. The day was declared a holiday for the citizens of Paris, crowned by a firework display on the place Louis XV (today's place de la Concorde). The fireworks, though, proved to be something of a damp squib, but much worse was to follow, when 132 people were crushed owing to poor crowd control and a movement of panic.

If there were fireworks on the wedding night, there certainly were none in the wedding chamber. The couple did not consummate the marriage for seven years, owing to a physical incompatibility that made sexual relations almost a painful impossibility. Nevertheless, much to the relief of the Bourbons and Habsburgs who wanted to see their military alliance confirmed with an heir, a child was born in 1778.

View of the Palais-Royal and its garden.

Unfortunately, it was a daughter, Marie-Thérèse. A male heir, Louis-Joseph, eventually followed in 1781.

The young – unhappy – couple were installed in the now dull rurality of Versailles. Paris, on the other hand, was still revelling in its role as the centre of the Enlightenment, in which writers and philosophers endlessly debated theories on reason and natural law in cafés such as Procope. News of the American Revolution in 1776 gave further fuel to these discussions.

In the centre of the city, the Palais-Royal, owned now by the king's cousin Louis Philippe II, Duke of Orléans, became the headquarters of a new form of hedonism. Beside the lavish royal residence, Philippe installed a wooden bazaar, renting out plots that housed cafés, gambling dens and brothels. By the end of the eighteenth century it had become one of the city's biggest attractions for visitors, and so crowded that it was known as 'the capital of Paris'. 'A prisoner could live there without getting bored and would dream of freedom only after several years,' noted the contemporary chronicler Louis-Sébastien Mercier about this 'beautiful Pandora's Box'. It also very quickly became the engine room of revolutionary politics.

Paris had been an open city since Louis XIV removed the last protective walls, but in 1780 the city closed in on itself once again. Louis XVI accepted the proposition to build the Fermiers généraux (tax farmers') walls, surrounding Paris not with military defences but rather with tax-generating barriers. This overly fancy enclosure consisting of 62 Neoclassical toll barriers designed by architect Claude Nicolas Ledoux, proved very unpopular, and not just because of its fiscal role. A later witticism summarized the Parisians' objection: 'Pour augmenter son numéraire / Et raccourcir notre horizon / La Ferme a jugé nécessaire / De mettre Paris en prison.' (To increase their cash / and reduce our horizons / the tax farmers have judged it / necessary to put Paris in prison.)

Despite such new means of generating income, the country's finances were in a perilous state. The monarchy – particularly Marie Antoinette herself – was seen by the people as corrupt, debauched and out of touch. The so-called Affair of the Diamond Necklace in 1785, in which the entirely innocent queen was accused of defrauding the crown jewellers of a vast sum of money, did not help matters. In a sign of just how critical things had become, the king called an emergency meeting of the Estates-General in Versailles in the spring of 1789. It was the first time that this assembly representing the nobles, the clergy and the third estate – the common bourgeoisie – had been brought together since 1614.

'We have need of a concourse of our faithful subjects, to assist us in surmounting all the difficulties we find relative to the state of our finances,' wrote Louis to the Estates, before assuring all participants that they would be able to 'confer and to record remonstrances, complaints and grievances'. The Estates-General was not able to agree on any solutions. Jacques Necker, the unpopular finance minister, tried to impose new taxes, but in exchange, the bourgeoisie demanded reforms that Louis was not prepared to accept. Instead, he sacked Necker, leaving himself with severe financial problems and no one to help him solve them. Fed up with the endless fruitless debates, the Third Estate

François Courboin, *A Gambling Hell in the Palais-Royal, Year VIII (1800)*, 1898, colour plate.

voted to split from the group and set up a National Assembly for the people. Louis slunk away from the meeting and fell into one of his regular bouts of depression. His actions at such times were ridiculed in a satirical rhyme: 'What need is there for me to think? When I can hunt and I can drink!' Pamphlets bearing such cutting texts were becoming ever more popular, and Marie Antoinette, for her part, was regularly portrayed as a lesbian partaking in drunken orgies. Perhaps more tellingly, in political circles she had also become known as Madame Deficit. The figures seemed to back up this soubriquet. In 1788 court expenditure accounted for 67 per cent of total national spending.

While these events were taking place in Versailles, Paris was becoming extremely twitchy. In April 1789 the ever-radical Faubourg Saint-Antoine ('France watched Paris, Paris watched the Faubourg Saint-Antoine,' Victor Hugo later noted in *Les Misérables*) came unstuck when riots in a wallpaper factory led to the deaths of one hundred people. A little further down the Faubourg, the Bastille prison was also becoming a focus. From his cell window, the writer the Marquis de Sade egged on the ever-increasing number of protesters, inventing tales of maltreatment and assassinations. Although the Bastille looked dreadful from the outside, the reality was a little different. The Marquis was in fact quite comfortably installed in two rooms, surrounded by his own furniture and a library. Possibly because of his troublemaking, he was transferred elsewhere shortly before the violence kicked off.

'Who knows what has happened at the Bastille, what it encloses, what it has enclosed,' exclaimed Mercier, underlining the prison's heavy symbolism. For Voltaire, who had been incarcerated there twice earlier in the eighteenth century, it

Jean-Pierre Houël, *The Storming of the Bastille*, 1789, watercolour.

was a palace of vengeance, and that reputation was further established through popular tales of torture and false imprisonment. Most famous of all was 'the man in the iron mask', a semi-mythical character 'of an out-of-the-ordinary size, young and of the most splendid and noble figure', mentioned by Voltaire in the 1770s.

On 14 July 1789 protesters attacked the Bastille and Les Invalides hospital, in search of weapons and grain that were said to be stored there. Similar information had also caused a group to attack the city's opera house, but they were extremely disappointed to discover that the weapons they found there – axes and clubs – were simply props made of cardboard.

At the Bastille, the mob was surprised to find only seven prisoners inside: four forgers, two lunatics and one deviant aristocrat placed there by his own family. Nevertheless, they set the symbolic building on fire, and killed the prison governor, the Marquis de Launay, before parading his head around the city on a stick.

Word of the insurrection quickly reached Louis in Versailles, who was told of the uprising by the Duke of Liancourt while still in bed. 'Is this a revolt?' the king enquired. 'No, sire, it is a revolution,' replied his adviser.

The event may well have marked the beginning of the French Revolution, but it was far from the end for Louis XVI. Three days later, on 17 July, he entered Paris to a rapturous reception from a crowd that thought he was ready to make reforms. Initial signs were good, as Louis granted certain powers to the new National Assembly. In a sign of the new order, the assembly issued the Declaration of the Rights of Man and of the Citizen on 26 August 1789.

The king made the fatal mistake of keeping his base in Versailles. He did not trust the powder keg that was Paris, but his absence from the city also made Parisians suspicious. Was he planning a counteroffensive from the traditional Bourbon base? In fact, his inaction was more a sign of his lack of character. He was, declared the American statesman Governor Morris later to Thomas Jefferson, 'the mildest monarch who ever filled the French throne'.

Putting an end to all doubt, in October an unlikely posse of women marched out to Versailles from Paris. They went ostensibly to demand grain and flour, but returned with Louis and Marie Antoinette in their baskets. Paris once again became the centre of power in the country, and the royal family and its entourage set themselves up in the Tuileries palace, where they were more or less under house arrest. Even while keeping him under close watch, Parisians were suspicious that Louis was still not supporting the Revolution, a sentiment that only increased after the royal family's some-what comical escape attempt in June 1791. The plan had been carefully thought out, but Marie Antoinette, disguised as a servant, delayed the escape by getting lost in the streets of Paris. When the royal coach did eventually get away, bad luck – and a sharp eye – caught the party out. Attempting to reach the Royalist stronghold of Varennes in the northeast of France, the king was unmasked thanks to a postmaster's son who recognized him from the face of a coin.

Although a kingless republic had not been the goal in 1789, Louis' escape attempt brought that eventuality closer to reality. The purpose of the Revolution was initially a constitutional monarchy, but for many this now seemed impossible. On 10 August 1792 a mob stormed the Tuileries, forcing the royal family to seek shelter in the National Assembly. This may have been a particularly stressful day for the royal family, but it did not prevent Louis from eating a dinner that consisted of two soups, eight starters, four roasts and eight desserts two days later.

The next day the National Assembly debated and eventually voted to force the king to abdicate. Creating the first French Republic was not enough, though. The 'arrogant, conceited, handsome' Louis-Antoine de Saint-Just, one of the new radical rulers, insisted that the king should be executed, not for what he had done but for what he represented. 'A man cannot reign innocently,' he pointed out, cranking the Revolution up to the next level.

Almost immediately, Paris descended into bloodthirsty chaos. Over four days at the beginning of September, a mob went on the rampage, massacring prisoners, prostitutes and the insane in the city's prisons and hospitals. In total, 1,300 people were killed. For revolutionary leaders such as Maximilien Robespierre, this was simply 'the will of the people' being expressed.

The Convention, the first incarnation of the Republic, became a battle between the Girondins – moderates who were inherently suspicious of Paris – and the pro-Parisian Montagnards, who included Robespierre, Georges Danton and Jean-Paul Marat. This trio believed that the Revolution could be a success only if it were extreme and radical, and that the most militant people of Paris – the sans-culottes – would be the great deciders. 'Citizens, did you want a revolution without a revolution?' asked Robespierre in a speech at the Convention Nationale on 5 November 1792.

Splits within the Republican political elite became even more evident at the trial of Louis XVI. A majority voted for execution – including his own cousin, the Duke of Orléans. Louis was eventually beheaded on 21 January 1793; Marie Antoinette followed on 16 October. Her final letter implored her sister to 'let my son never forget his father's last words . . . never try to avenge our deaths.' Louis-Charles would not get the opportunity, however. Aged ten, he died on 8 June 1795 in the Temple, officially of tuberculosis, but almost certainly of an illness exacerbated by damp conditions and neglect.

With the balance of power careering headfirst into radicalism, the Girondins were expelled from Paris, and some leaders were executed owing to their lack of revolutionary zeal. The Convention was now firmly under the control of the sans-culottes, who introduced sweeping social reform – and a regime of state terror. Their new toy was the guillotine, an invention that had first been tested on sheep and the corpses of criminals at the Bicêtre hospital in 1792. It supposedly offered a more humane execution, but really it was chosen because it sped up the process so that more people could be killed.

France adopted a new revolutionary calendar with secular, agrarian names, and across Paris religious buildings were deconsecrated and pressed into use as grain stores or marketplaces. Church land – along with that of the aristocracy – was confiscated, and the whole nomenclature of the city began to change. Royal statues and royal place names were removed, along with anything related to religion. Out at Saint-Denis, the royal tombs were desecrated, and the remains placed in a communal pit.

The Terror ended after about 17,000 beheadings in 1794, perhaps inevitably with the execution of the person who had pushed it the furthest: Robespierre. He had encouraged the Parisian mob to rebel, but it eventually cost him his own head. 'The republic! It is lost because the brigands have triumphed,' he declared in despair just before his execution.

The Republic was not immediately lost. The Convention became the Directory, a feeble bourgeois institution in a city tired of power struggles and executions. Growing ever more confident, the Royalists attempted a comeback, but were defeated in the Coup du 18 brumaire (9 November 1799) by a young general called Napoléon Bonaparte, fresh from military success in Italy and Egypt. After the chaos and panic of the Terror, and the comparative boredom of the Directory, the new leader brought a bit of glamour back to Paris, mostly thanks to his wife, Joséphine. Six years older than Napoléon, she had been married to another general, who had been executed during the Revolution.

Just a few weeks after being sworn in as First Consul of the new Consulate government, Napoléon was off on another military adventure. In the entire length of his reign, he would be in Paris for only about one thousand days. The couple had set up home in the Tuileries palace, but Joséphine never felt comfortable there: 'I will never be happy here,' she said. 'I can feel the queen's ghost asking what I am doing in her bed.'

Despite his frequent absences, Paris was something of an obsession for Napoléon. He had arrived in the city as a young man to become a soldier, and it was at the Palais-Royal that he lost his virginity (to a prostitute, as did many young men). Declaring that 'men are only great through the monuments

Louis Léopold Boilly, *The Public Viewing David's 'Coronation' at the Louvre*, 1810, oil on canvas.

they leave behind them,' he wanted to build, but few projects were finished during his reign.

After Napoléon had crowned himself emperor on 2 December 1804, his goal was to create a suitably imperial city. The Louvre became the Musée Napoléon, and was quickly crammed full of treasures pillaged during the emperor's European adventures. Vivant Denon, its curator, justified the thievery by declaring, somewhat disingenuously, that France was 'the only country in the world which could provide an inviolable asylum to these masterpieces'. In other words, Paris was doing everyone a favour by holding them in safekeeping.

Despite such grandiosity and with building works rarely leaving the drawing board, Napoléon's most important and lasting achievements were the practical changes he made to the city. He helped to create a civil code – which is still largely in use today – and the Banque de France, but his most popular development was something simpler. When he asked his advisers what he could leave behind that would be both useful and lasting, he was told: 'Water'. He quickly made the decision to build a canal, and installed dozens of fountains across the city.

After divorcing the infertile Joséphine, Napoléon married Marie-Louise of Austria (astonishingly, Marie Antoinette's niece). The marriage was a political arrangement, but also a practical one for a man desperate for an heir: 'C'est un ventre que j'épouse' – 'It's a womb I'm marrying' – he charmingly declared. But it worked. On 20 March 1811 Paris discovered the sex of Napoléon's firstborn. After 22 bursts of cannon fire, cheers rang out in the streets – boys were celebrated with 101 bursts, while girls had only had 21. His son was quickly proclaimed king of Rome and given the soubriquet Aiglon, little eagle. Napoléon's first big successes – expanding his empire across Europe and out towards Asia and Africa – turned into ever heavier defeats on the eastern front. After the first major European conflict, the battle of the nations in Leipzig in 1813, Allied forces marched on Paris to bring an end to the reign of the scourge of the continent.

Paris had not been occupied by foreign troops since the fifteenth century, and had not experienced any kind of warfare since the Fronde in 1652, but in March 1814 the Allied forces entered Paris. On 6 April Napoléon was forced to abdicate, and he was exiled to the Mediterranean island of Elba.

The fall of Napoléon paved the way for the return of the monarchy, in particular the Bourbon dynasty, and Louis XVI's brother was installed as Louis XVIII (the uncrowned Louis XVII, Louis-Charles, had died in the Temple). However, the initial reign of Louis XVIII, who had been out of France since 1791, was a very short one. Napoléon quickly escaped from Elba and marched back to Paris, forcing Louis XVIII to flee the country once again. After building up another army, the ever more bellicose and erratic Napoléon went off to his final defeat at the Battle of Waterloo. Paris was invaded once again by the Allied forces, despite spirited resistance during a sixteen-day siege.

Louis XVIII returned, this time to reign for nine years. The new king rejected Versailles, instead setting himself up in the Tuileries, where he even slept in Napoléon's bed. Next to the palace, the Louvre became, as the Scottish novelist Walter Scott wrote to his sister, 'truly doleful to look at . . . the place full of dust', after France was ordered to return its looted treasures. The newly restored monarchy was itself cheerless; the obese Louis XVIII, suffering from gout and dropsy, moved so little that he gave himself the nickname 'le roi fauteil' (the armchair king). He died in September 1824, the last French monarch to expire on the throne. He was succeeded by his brother Charles x, the last grandson of Louis xv, already nearly seventy years old. Autocratic and pro-clerical, Charles proved extremely unpopular, especially when he tried to claim extra powers for the Crown and clamped down on freedom of the press. His most significant action was an external one: the annexation of Algeria, then the world's tenth largest nation.

Paris remained a desperately divided city. A report from 1829 declared 136,000 of the 224,000 households in Paris to be officially 'poor', and it was not a great surprise to see such misery turn against the king. The three-day revolt known as the *Trois Glorieuses* took place on 27–29 July 1830. As the troubles began, Charles declared: 'I see no middle way between the throne and the scaffold,' but he still escaped to exile in England, before later dying of cholera in the Austrian Empire in 1836. He remains the only French king to be buried outside France.

The July Revolution was a rapid and relatively calm one that hardly interrupted the flow of the city. Writing from his study in Paris on 28 July, the composer Hector Berlioz noted that 'the sound of the cannon and of the gunfire was extremely favourable to my latest piece' (*La Mort de Sardanapale*).

'What the people need now is a popular king surrounded by Republican institutions,' declared the Marquis de Lafayette, an aristocrat and veteran of the American Revolutionary War. Louis-Philippe (son of Louis-Philippe, Duke of Orléans, who had supported the execution of Louis xvi) tried hard to be

Aux Merveilleux

Merveilleux & Incroyables

4 parts	14,40 €
6 parts	21,60 €
8 parts	28,80 €

A slice of post-revolutionary Paris: Aux Merveilleux de Fred patisserie,
rue du pont Louis-Philippe.

INCROYABLES AND MERVEILLEUSES

As the French Revolution slid quietly into the more sedate Directory, a strange subculture emerged in Paris. Surviving aristocrats and their offspring came out of hiding and began to dance again, at events known as the *bals des victimes*: 'To be admitted to the feast and the dance, you had to show a certificate proving that you had lost a father, a mother, a husband, a wife, a brother or a sister under the iron of the guillotine.'

Taking the floor were the *merveilleuses*, young women obsessed with ancient Greece, with 'naked arms, the breast uncovered, feet in sandals, hair twisted in braids around their heads', and the *incroyables*, extravagant dandies in bouffant scarves and tight trousers. They represented the *jeunesse dorée*, aristocratic youth with a desperate urge to spend their precociously inherited fortunes before the wind turned against them once more.

As well as dancing, they adopted a number of strange habits. They refused to pronounce the letter 'R' (because of its reference to 'Revolution'), and would often wear red ribbons around their necks, transforming the mark of the guillotine into a decorative accessory. It is not clear if this was down to ghoulish humour or some kind of collective post-traumatic stress disorder.

The subculture provided inspiration in the 1980s for the patissière Frédéric Vaucamps, who transformed a traditional recipe of meringue and cream cakes from the north of France into a creation he called 'les merveilleux'. Vaucamp, who draws comparisons between the lightness of his cakes and the insouciance of the Directory's gilded youth, today sells the cakes at several shops in Paris. If this seems, like the *incroyables* and the *merveilleuses*, a little frivolous, be assured that the cakes at least are in very good taste.

Léopold Morice, *Trois Glorieuses*, 1883, bronze relief on the Monument of the Republic, place de la République.

that popular monarch, but could never quite manage it. He would wander the streets of Paris with a green umbrella and two sets of gloves, one for shaking the hands of the rich, another for the poor.

Perhaps unsurprisingly, after the upheaval of the previous forty years, Louis-Philippe was severely lacking in confidence, and constantly questioned the legitimacy of his own role. Rather than starting anything anew, he chose to finish earlier projects. He helped to complete the Arc de Triomphe and the church of the Madeleine – both Napoléon's projects – and was even instrumental in bringing the body of the emperor back to Paris in 1840.

Paris, encouraged by a new breed of bourgeois bankers, became a place of speculation, shopping and consuming, with the development of elegant commercial passageways and the first *grands magasins* department stores. Sharing this middle-class playground, though, was an ever greater number of workers in the poorer areas of the city, 'compressed together by poverty, stifled by necessity, drowned in drink, worn out by strong liquor', as Honoré de Balzac put it. The poor had no voice in the new city, but they did have champions. Since

Louis-Philippe rarely exercised censorship, Balzac, Victor Hugo, Gustave Flaubert and Alexandre Dumas were free to write about all parts of society, but it was the poor who inspired these Romantics the most, providing a backdrop to the era of the great French novel.

The existence of such a divided society was bound to make Louis-Philippe unpopular, and he suffered a total of seven assassination attempts during his reign. In 1840–44, becoming ever more paranoid – with good reason, perhaps – he created a huge ring of defences around Paris, known as the Thiers fortifications. By 1847 the situation was becoming critical for the king. In an attempt to restrict large gatherings, he banned public meetings in the city, but in true Parisian style, such meetings were simply replaced by banquets, which had no such restrictions. The public revolts prompted Alexis de Toqueville in January 1848 to declare to parliament that Paris was 'sleeping on a volcano', but that same month Louis-Philippe was still confident enough to tell an assembled group of ambassadors at his new year's greeting that two things were now impossible in Europe: war and revolution. One month later he was overthrown.

After a thousand hectic, glorious, divisive, warmongering years, the French monarchy had sputtered to an end. Its final figurehead scuttled away incognito to England under the name Mr Smith.

6 Rebuilding and Repression

With the monarchy at an end, the French might have been expected to look forwards. Instead, at the beginning of the Second Republic they chose a nephew of Napoléon, Louis-Napoléon Bonaparte, as their new president. At first it was assumed that his leadership would be temporary – the ever-plotting Adolphe Thiers called him 'a cretin whom we will manage' – but although Thiers did later succeed him, that was not for another 23 years. That Louis-Napoléon actually made it into power at all was already a great surprise. Physically far less intimidating than his imperial uncle, and without an ounce of his charisma, he was also tainted by previous failure: twice he had tried to organize uprisings against Louis-Philippe by attacking garrison towns, but these rather feeble attempts were easily put down, and Louis-Napoléon was captured and sentenced to life imprisonment. He escaped to exile in London, where he developed an obsession with a certain English model of garden cities, parks, squares and working sanitation.

Louis-Napoléon came to power mostly thanks to changes to the electoral system. For the first time, universal male suffrage was in force, and the agricultural workers and petit bourgeois in small towns, who still represented the vast majority of the country, were mostly favourable to someone who offered a throwback to imperial glory. Louis-Napoléon proved far less popular in Paris, but for once the capital had to accept the choice of the provincials.

After three unspectacular years as president, Louis-Napoléon organized a *coup d'état* on the night of 1–2 December 1851, a date carefully chosen as the anniversary of the Battle of Austerlitz and his uncle's coronation. His justification for the action was that it headed off a Royalist uprising that was brewing in the country. 'My duty', he declared in a message to the population, 'is to thwart their perfidious projects, to maintain the Republic, and to save the country, by invoking the solemn judgment of the only sovereign that I acknowledge in France: the People!'

Others, however, could not help noticing that Louis-Napoléon was coming to the end of his term as president and was legally forbidden from standing for office again. Paris immediately protested and laid out its familiar barricades, but it was too little too late. Some 215 people were killed in street battles, but in reality they were fighting against both Louis-Napoléon and the will of the rest of the country. The people of Paris would file this defeat in the book of grievances, ready to be wielded in the future. On 20 December a national plebiscite confirmed Louis-Napoléon – with a vast majority – as the country's second emperor. He was crowned a year later, on the same significant date, and named himself Napoléon iii. (The second Napoléon – Bonaparte's son, 'the Aiglon' – had died in Austria in 1832.)

On 23 June 1853 Napoléon iii made perhaps the most important decision of his reign by appointing Georges-Eugène Haussmann his prefect for the Paris region. Napoléon iii had big – costly – plans for Paris, and needed by his side a visionary he could trust. The previous prefect, Jean-Jacques Berger, had eschewed Parisian immortality through excessive cautiousness, declaring: 'I'm certainly not going to be involved in the city's financial ruin.'

Haussmann was not afraid to spend money. As a Protestant from Alsace, he had organizational skills that more than covered his lack of flamboyance. His long-time associate in Paris, the engineer Jean-Charles Alphand, pointed out that he 'was perhaps not an orator, as he had neither a powerful voice nor the rousing eloquence that moves the masses'. Nevertheless, Haussmann always managed to encourage people towards 'immense action through his incomparable logic'.

Haussmann was a formidable administrator and financial manager, but significantly, he had no training in architecture. Rather than a builder, he preferred to describe himself as a 'demolition artist'. He agreed with Napoléon III that the reshaping of Paris would begin with the ripping-out of its old – and, to the two men, thoroughly rotten – heart. The pair would change the face of Paris completely, giving the city the appearance it still bears today, not to mention the many other cities around the world that copied the style. To achieve this, Napoléon III ensured that Haussmann had full powers to complete his projects, including compulsory purchasing and expropriations. All projects were decided by decree, too, rather than by discussion and vote.

At first the projects cost very little. Haussmann could buy up properties cheaply, demolish them and complete the renovation of the district, and then sell the land at much higher prices. However, the French parliament changed the game, insisting that he share his profits with the previous owners of the property. This forced him to take out huge loans to complete his schemes, and it would take the city of Paris a century to pay off its debts.

One of Haussmann's first projects was the clearing of the slums that for centuries had squeezed themselves up against the eastern end of the Louvre. It was a necessary embellishment for many observers, not least Honoré de Balzac, who had imagined the desperation of the Louvre in his book *La Cousine Bette* (Cousin Bette). In this area, described in the novel as 'the intimate alliance of the misery and splendour that characterize the queen of capitals', the Louvre cries out: 'Get those warts off my face!' Haussmann was only too happy to perform the surgery.

Less successful was his massacre of the cradle of Paris, the Île de la Cité. As a child, Haussmann had walked across the island on his way to school, and he remembered it in his memoirs as a 'place of thieves and murderers'. He delighted in knocking down the old buildings, which he 'had the joy of razing completely', but to the detriment of the character of the island, he left in their place just 'a barracks, a church, a hospital and a palace'.

Napoléon III, France's surprising second emperor.

Busy, modern Paris, though, became a thoroughly bewildering place for many. 'The Parisian finds himself disorientated in this Paris that is no longer Parisian,' noted the writer and critic Edmond de Goncourt, while Victor Hugo remarked later that it was too English – although fortunately, he pointed out, without the associated weather. Others felt that everything was moving too fast. In his poem 'Perte d'Auréole' (The Emergence of the Dandy, written in 1869 and published posthumously), Baudelaire wrote of the 'moving chaos where death comes at a gallop from all sides at once'.

Paris was already one of Europe's largest cities, but in 1860 the Empire doubled the size of the city by absorbing a number

PICTURES FROM THE PAST

Paris in the 1850s was, according to the historian Graham Robb, 'the dawn of the visible past', the period when the city was first dimly captured for posterity. Previously romanticized in sketches and paintings, Paris was revealed in its reality by the nascent art of photography, which handily emerged just when the city was on the cusp of a comprehensive facelift.

'It would be difficult to imagine what Paris was like before 1850 without the photos of Charles Marville,' wrote Patrice de Moncan in his book of photographs that compares the pre-Haussmannian city with today's Paris, but all concerned in Marville's work were fully aware of the impact these pictures would have. Marville began his photographic career by snapping the wedding decorations of Napoléon III and Eugénie in 1853, and then recording the baptism of the emperor's son, Eugène-Louis. After operating as the photographer of the 'imperial museum of the Louvre', he was named official photographer of the city of Paris in 1858.

Marville found himself confronted by a massive task, essentially one of the first acts of photographic propaganda: 'to show the misery of Paris and, through this, to justify the work of Haussmann and the immense upheaval engaged by the Empire.' The job eventually involved 425 shots taken over three years. Many of these photos and negatives have been preserved in the city's archives, and they feature eerie streets empty of people. This was not because they were not there – Paris in the 1850s was a densely populated place – but since exposure times were about fifteen minutes per photo, it was impossible to capture anything moving.

Marville's own history was more complicated. For many years nobody knew exactly when he had died or where he had been buried. It was only when recent research revealed that he had understandably changed his name from Charles-François Bossu (*bossu* is French for hunchback) – without changing any of his official papers – that these mysteries were solved.

The eerie streets of Charles Marville's Paris: *Rue Tirechape, de la rue St Honoré* – demolished to make way for the rue de Rivoli, *c.* 1853–70.

of suburban villages and towns. This move, primarily designed to increase the city's budget, involved the demolition of the Fermiers généraux wall, the city's boundary since 1784, and the grabbing of territory stretching out to the Thiers fortifications. 'They have sewn rags on to the dress of a queen,' said the city administrator Louis Lazare about this absorption of the mostly rural and shabby towns and villages, but it did push the population of Paris up towards two million.

Such a population rise meant an even greater need for suitable housing, but the empire did not take the opportunity to use its newly claimed territories to increase equality. Haussmann demolished 20,000 homes in the poorest, most central parts of Paris, replacing them with 40,000 new ones mostly along his new boulevards. However, while the middle classes happily moved from the now demolished districts to the smarter, more modern streets, their poorer ex-neighbours were not able to rent lodgings in the new Paris. The new outer districts of Paris – which were free of Haussmannian embellish-ment – thus became home to the displaced workers, some of whom were pushed even further out into the wild and rural suburbs. This accumulation of resentful workers, away from the glitter and comforts of the empire, would soon prove extremely dangerous.

With the poor swept away, the Second Empire was a bourgeois fête, but also a party that was extremely hypocrit-ical in nature. In 1857 Flaubert was prosecuted for obscenity after publishing *Madame Bovary* (he was acquitted), and in 1863 Édouard Manet was attacked for the immorality of his painting *Luncheon on the Grass*. At the same time, Napoléon III was paying 50,000 francs a month to his mistress the Comtesse de Castiglione.

For Napoléon III, the Universal Exhibition of 1867 provided an opportunity to show off his modern metropolis. He had organized an exhibition in 1855 – a rapid response to the Great Exhibition held in London in 1851 – but this time the new city was ready for its visitors. The guest list was long, but it included such ominous visitors as Kaiser Wilhelm and Otto von Bismarck from Prussia.

The emperor and Haussmann took Kaiser Wilhelm and the tsar of Russia on a tour of the new Paris. The tsar was suitably flattering: 'Before this queen that is Paris, we are but simple bourgeois,' he declared. Wilhelm was less subtle. Surveying the panorama from the top of the Buttes-Chaumont park, he pointed to a spot in the distance and spluttered: 'There's the gateway through which we entered Paris in 1815!' Embarrassed, Haussmann quickly replied: 'We have built some fortifications since.' Wilhelm's remark was possibly a joke, but certainly a warning.

Struggling both politically and financially, the empire approached the end of the decade in a seemingly terminal decline. In 1869 Napoléon hosted what turned out to be the final party at the Tuileries, with the Empress Eugénie dressed – somewhat unwisely – as Marie Antoinette. She did not lose her head, but her husband lost his right-hand man. Elections later in the year saw a victory for the liberals, and Baron

An early photograph by Charles Marville, *Rue Haute des Ursins de la rue St Landry*, c. 1853.

Haussmann was ungratefully sacrificed. Seeking to salvage some kind of glory, Napoléon set out on a hopeless campaign against the Prussians. The conflict was sparked vaguely by disagreement over the succession to the Spanish throne, and partly by Bismarck's criticism of France in the press. 'The liberal empire goes to war on a mere point of etiquette,' was the *Illustrated London News*'s succinct headline.

War broke out in July 1870, but by September Napoléon III had surrendered, following defeat at the Battle of Sedan. Imperial, frivolous France had been swatted aside by the scientific and mechanical Prussians. On 4 September the Second Empire came to an end and the Third Republic was proclaimed.

With Napoléon III in captivity, Victor Hugo – who had spent the entire Second Empire in exile – was safe to return. Entering France from Belgium, he despaired when he saw the misery of the beaten army. 'I should have preferred never to return', he declared, 'rather than to see France so humiliated.' With the Prussians advancing on the French capital, Hugo wrote the invaders a letter, imploring them to spare 'Paris . . . la ville des villes.' By the time he arrived at Paris's Gare du Nord railway station, his grandiloquence had risen to another level. Met off his train by a large crowd, he declared: 'Defend Paris, guard Paris. Saving Paris is more than saving France, it's saving the world. Paris is the very centre of humanity. Paris is the sacred city. He who attacks Paris makes a mass attack on the entire human race.'

Not to be deterred, Bismarck and the Prussians continued to Paris and laid siege to the city. Already defeated, the rest of France wanted to sign an armistice with the Germans, but Paris voted to continue the war. Ominously, the siege began just as a freezing winter was setting in, and when the Prussians took Versailles, Paris was effectively cut off from the rest of the country. The ingenious Parisians managed to break through – or rather over – the Prussian lines by building and flying hot-air balloons, although they could only take messages and people out of Paris, and bring nothing into the city. A lack of piloting skills brought other problems, with one balloon ending up in Norway. With nothing coming into the city, the starving citizens were forced to eat dogs, cats, rats and the animals in the zoo.

Hugo noted in his diary that 'patés of rat are being made. They are said to be very good,' and was given joints of bear, deer and antelope from the city's menagerie in the Jardin des Plantes. All the animals were fair game, apart from lions and tigers, which were thought too dangerous to kill, and monkeys, which were declared to be too similar to man.

As an additional humiliation to the invaded nation, on 18 January Kaiser Wilhelm declared himself emperor of a now united Germany in the Galerie des Glaces at Versailles, under Charles Le Brun's paintings celebrating the victories of Louis XIV on the Rhine. It was a carefully planned and staged insult that would poison Franco–German relations for 75 years. Fearing for his safety in the face of proletarian pressure, the president of the Government of National Defence, General Trochu, sought an immediate peace treaty with the Prussians. It would be an extremely tough deal: the loss of Alsace and Lorraine, compensation running into billions of francs and – with a touch of spiteful sadism – the marching of Prussian troops up and down the Champs-Élysées.

'During four months . . . patriotic Paris had . . . accepted all: pestilence, assault, pillage, everything except capitulation,' noted the journalist Prosper-Olivier Lissagaray. The people of Paris were furious about the surrender, and refused to accept the treaty. The dispute came to a head at Montmartre when the army tried to seize 171 pieces of artillery that the National Guard had amassed for the defence of the city. It had been built in Paris, and the people of the city claimed it as their own. The soldiers were beaten back, and returned to Versailles, where Thiers had set up an acting government. Left to its own devices, Paris set up the Commune as a rival power, prompting Thiers to launch a second siege of the city, this time observed from a distance by the Prussians. On 10 March a resolution was passed declaring that Paris was no longer the capital of France. The centre of the country had moved back once again to Versailles.

The Paris Commune represented the first claiming of power by the working classes since the beginning of the Industrial Revolution, and was therefore viewed with interest by people around the world. Many came to observe from neighbouring countries, and some from even further. 'The attraction of rebellious Paris was so strong that men hurried thither from America to behold this spectacle unprecedented in the world's history – the greatest town of the European continent in the hands of the proletariat,' wrote Lissagaray in his fiery *History of the Paris Commune*.

This political spectacle soon became more dramatic, notably on 2 April when government troops began shelling Paris. In its quest to reclaim Paris, the French government was assisted by Prussian forces, who freed 60,000 French prisoners in exchange for even tougher conditions of peace. 'Of all M. Thiers's crimes,' declared Lissagaray, 'one of the most odious will certainly be his introducing the conquerors of France into our civil discords and begging their help in order to crush Paris.'

Although the Commune had an unclear leadership structure and an over-profusion of sometimes contradictory goals, at its heart was a claim 'for the largest and most enlightened city of France [to have] at least the rights enjoyed by the smallest village.' Since Paris had been synonymous with national power, it had rarely had its own unique structure and leadership. Indeed, those in charge seemed unsure about what that might entail. The Commune had negotiated finance with the Banque de France ('it is not my business to judge events,' said the bank's governor), but made no use of Paris's other advantages. 'All diplomats of Europe dreaded the opening of the portfolios at the foreign office,' noted Lissagaray, but there is no evidence that the leaders of Paris even looked at the documents. Despite rumours spread by the government, the Commune did not confiscate and sell art, but simply contented itself with the destruction of Thiers' Paris home and the sharing of his property among city hospitals.

With government troops approaching, and discussions among Commune leaders ever more fraught, the movement

9. PARIS — Souvenir de l'année terrible 1870-71
Barricade Rue Lafayette et Faubourg St-Martin C. M.
18 Mars 1871

Barricade at the rue Lafayette and Faubourg Saint-Martin.

veered towards anarchy. The Archbishop of Paris was seized and held prisoner, and much time and effort was put into the pulling down of Napoléon Bonaparte's column in the place Vendôme (the painter Gustave Courbet would later be charged for this action, but he escaped to Switzerland before he could be punished).

The crushing of the Commune began on Sunday 21 May 1871, the first day of a period known forever afterwards as the *Semaine sanglante* (Bloody Week). Government troops entered the city – which, strangely, was completely undefended – while Parisians attended a concert at the Tuileries palace. Lissagaray noted this discrepancy carefully: 'The bright spring dresses of the women lit up the green alleys; people eagerly inhaled the fresh air sent forth from the great trees. Two hundred yards off, on the place de la Concorde, the Versailles shells burst.' The following day 70,000 troops poured into the western districts of the city, where they were largely welcomed by the mostly bourgeois population. The Communards began building barricades in the centre, believing that they would

Rue de Rivoli after the fires of the Paris Commune, May 1871.

have the advantage in hand-to-hand street fighting ('Paris, with its barricades, is undefeatable,' declared the city's Committee of Public Safety).

Women had been at the forefront of the Commune, and a women's battalion led by Louise Michel attempted valiantly to defend Montmartre before being beaten back. Faced with such stiff resistance, Thiers launched the systematic rounding-up and executing of Communards – even of any woman found with an empty bottle in her hand. Chillingly, the new Haussmannian green spaces – notably the Monceau and Buttes-Chaumont parks – became favoured killing grounds.

Buildings across the city caught fire, including the Hôtel de Ville and the Tuileries palace, although it was not always clear if this was a deliberate action by the Communards or the result of government cannon. 'It seemed literally as if the whole town was on fire,' the terrified English seed merchant

Edwin Child noted in a letter; he had rather unluckily found himself trapped in Paris during the Franco-Prussian War, and was still stuck there during the Commune.

With government troops massively outnumbering the Communards, the last pockets of fighters were pushed into the east of the city, around the Père Lachaise cemetery, where, Lissagaray observed, the two sides fought 'frightful hand-to-hand scuffles' in which 'foes rolled and died in the same grave'. By the end of the week the conflict was over. About 25,000 people had been killed, and thousands more would shortly be exiled to the French territory of New Caledonia in the South Pacific.

Around Paris, wrote the novelist and critic Théophile Gautier, 'a silence of death reigned on the ruins.' Not even the song of a single bird, he noted, could be heard.

7 The Belle Époque

A little more than a month after the Commune had reached its tragic and brutal conclusion, visitors were already back in Paris, now taking tours of the charred ruins. 'You have to see them,' wrote the journalist Ludovic Hans in his hastily put-together *Guide à travers les ruines de Paris* (A Guide Through the Paris Ruins, 1871), 'you have to observe for yourself what delirium can achieve, served by nameless people in its service.' This seemed designed to mask a genuine fascination (shared by most visitors) with the twisted, burned, crumbling appearance of a city that had wilfully destroyed itself.

At 16 rue Royale, Hans noted, 'the flames destroyed a boulangerie that made croissants that the employees of the (nearby) Marine Ministry will never forget.' He needn't have been concerned. This bakery, which had been opened in 1862 by Louis Ernest Ladurée, reopened as an even more bourgeois tea shop and purveyor of macaroons. 'A fire in the bakery opened the opportunity to transform it into a pastry shop,' declares the official Ladurée website today, artfully neglecting to mention the revolutionary origin of the flames.

As did the Ladurée shop, Paris would once again bounce back remarkably quickly from adversity. The Commune was a spectacular parenthesis, but it could not mask the fact that France still owed a war indemnity of 5 billion francs to Prussia. For the German chancellor Otto von Bismarck, this massive sum was a way of emptying the coffers of and silencing 'the richest country in Europe', but the result was not what he expected.

Édouard Detaille, *Inauguration of the Paris Opera House, 5 January 1875*, print from an original painting, *c.* 1878, gouache on paper.

By September 1873, two years before the deadline, France had paid off its war debt and was on the road to recovery.

The new Third Republic was charged with rebuilding a city and a nation, but it also concerned itself with creating a new moral order and repositioning religion at the centre of people's lives. For Parisians, this was symbolized by the construction of the Sacré-Coeur de Montmartre in expiation of the sins of the Commune (although the bulbous church would not be officially opened until 1923). The Hôtel de Ville was also swiftly rebuilt – as a faithful replica – and Napoléon Bonaparte was replaced on top of the column in the place Vendôme.

After much delay, Charles Garnier's Opéra building was also finally opened in 1875, but the ceremony was in keeping with the frugality of the times. 'Mr Charles Garnier had to pay 120 francs for his box on the second floor,' wrote *Le Figaro* in its report on the opening concert. The refusal of the minister of culture to give him free entry was even more surprising considering that the architect was still working on finishing touches to the building two hours before the curtain was raised.

Despite having hounded out Haussmann and Napoléon III, the politicians running the Third Republic were happy to continue almost all the two men's projects – and with increased vigour. Between 1878 and 1888 three times as many buildings were put up in Paris as were constructed in 1860–69. The focus on convenience and comfort fitted the ideals of the Republic, but the authorities wasted little time on designing new models. Most of these new buildings adhered to a set blueprint that 'minimized the idiosyncratic and maximized the standard' – as well as maximizing the profits.

As a contrast to the efficient drabness of the Third Republic, Impressionist painters brought splashes of vibrant colour to Paris. After taking refuge from the Franco-Prussian War, Claude Monet and Camille Pissarro returned from dank, foggy London and were inspired by Paris's new *joie de vivre*. 'One morning, one of us, having no black, used blue instead, and Impressionism was born,' Pierre-Auguste Renoir told the art critic Gustave Coquiot, reclaiming a term that had originally been used as an insult.

Camille Pissarro, *Boulevard Montmartre, Morning, Cloudy Weather*, 1897, oil on canvas.

In 1874 the Société anonyme des artistes peintres, sculpteurs et graveurs, a movement created by artists including Monet, Renoir and Edgar Degas, held its first exhibition in the studio of the photographer Nadar. The critic and humorist Louis Leroy, describing the 'hard day' he spent at the event, labelled the show 'L'Exposition des Impressionnistes' after examining Monet's painting *Impression, Sunrise*: 'Impression, I was sure of it. I said to myself that since I'm impressed there must be some impression in there . . . And what freedom, what ease in the craftsmanship! Embryonic wallpaper is more finished than this maritime scene.' Nevertheless, Paris would soon come to be defined by the works of this group, their paintings of street-scapes and railway stations, of leisurely Sundays by the river or of riotous and fevered nights in the cabarets of Montmartre, the old village that the bohemians had transformed into a year-round carnival.

The 1880s began with a significant landmark: Victor Hugo's eightieth birthday. The great man had become the father of the nation, the man – literally – of the nineteenth century. Indeed, so famous and respected was he that the city authorities changed the name of the street on which he lived to boulevard Victor Hugo. On the day of his birthday, it was estimated that 600,000 people marched past his apartment to give him their best wishes.

Hugo died five years later. He had requested that his body should be taken to his grave in a pauper's hearse with no religious ceremony, but the government instead decided on a state funeral and a place among the *grands hommes* in the Panthéon. His embalmed body lay in his bed for eight days before being taken to lie in state overnight under the Arc de Triomphe, guarded by twelve young poets. The following day it was paraded through Paris in front of two million people, before being placed in the Panthéon. The whole event lasted more than eight hours.

Filling Hugo's large shoes as champion of the Parisians was Émile Zola, whose vision of the city was even darker. This marked the triumph of Naturalism over Romanticism, a movement Zola had ridiculed in *Le Ventre de Paris* (The Belly of Paris, 1873): 'They're always saying the same thing: "You can't create art out of science"; "Industry kills poetry", and so on.' For the Naturalists, industry – the 'vast expanse' of the Saint-Lazare railway station, for example, with the 'copper-coloured disc of the sun' descending through its haze – was poetry.

Zola saw beauty everywhere around him in Paris, and he observed and noted everything carefully. He recorded snippets of conversation, mapped the changing city and even introduced familiar brands into his writing. It was a completely new style of literature. 'For the first time,' noted the critic Robert Abirached in a preface to a later edition of Zola's *Le Ventre de Paris*, 'a writer understood and assumed responsibility for the beauty of the modern urban landscape.'

Such murky realism and portrayal of the underbelly of Paris were not to everyone's taste, however. For many critics, it was a virtuosity that was 'empty' and 'detestable', representing a new society where 'the interior world no longer exists'. Gone was the introspection of the Romantics; everything was now firmly on the surface.

Most definitely on the surface was the 'inutile et monstreuse' (useless and monstrous) Eiffel Tower, star of the Universal Exhibition of 1889. It celebrated the rise of function, production and science, and the industrialization of Paris, but to many it also objectified the decline of beauty and grace. Faced by vitriolic critics, its architect, Gustave Eiffel, counter-attacked: 'Why should what is admirable in Egypt become hideous and ridiculous in Paris?' he asked. In any case, built in 27 months – on time and without any accidents – it was a triumph. The world's tallest tower, it was also a potent – and pointed – sign of the city's new-found confidence. By 1895 Paris was finally out of its post-war, post-Commune depression and enjoying a new golden age. Along with Great Britain and Germany, France had taken most advantage of the Industrial Revolution, and the three nations were making the rest of the world pay. Paris was becoming ever wealthier and more attractive, a world city of luxury shops and extravagant creativity.

The Parisian authorities began to throw off the most restrictive elements of Haussmannianism. The buildings were still constructed in long, straight lines and no taller than 20 m (66 ft), but new rules allowed the addition of decorative elements. Bow windows and curved turrets, carved facades and floral-themed ironwork sprouted on new buildings, the most visible element of the dominant but short-lived Art Nouveau movement.

Such decoration had also crept into the bars and cafés that were mushrooming across the city. In the late 1840s Paris possessed 4,500 such establishments, but by the 1880s, as the historian W. Scott Haine notes, there may have been as many as 42,000. By comparison, there were only 5,800 drinking establishments in London in the same period.

Many bars adopted what the writer Joris-Karl Huysmans called a 'false opulence', with their 'immense saloons, their ceilings covered in paintings, decorated with garlands, tiny flowers, of love scorched by the gas lights'. The Paris-based

The Eiffel Tower and Champ de Mars viewed from the Trocadéro Palace during the Universal Exhibition of 1889.

Visitors under the base of the Eiffel Tower, 1889.

American scholar Alvan F. Sanborn agreed that 'the furnishings are not in the best of taste; they are chiefly glitter and gaud', but he nevertheless declared such places to be 'a beautiful sight . . . so full of the brighter aspects of humanity.'

If on the Champs-Élysées or the Grands Boulevards these cafés were fashionable places in which to meet and be seen, in the poorer parts of the city – in Belleville, Menilmontant, Bastille – they were home to the city's first youth movement, the Apaches. Partly a myth created by the press, the name was nevertheless adopted by gangs of disaffected young men and women who followed specific dress codes – wide trousers, flat caps and, most of all, extravagant shoes: 'The height of Apache vanity was a pair of freshly polished pointed yellow boots with golden buttons.'

As were its cafés, the Paris of the Belle Époque was split into rich and poor, fashionable and unfashionable, but France as a whole was divided in other ways. The most notable example was the Dreyfus Affair, which began in 1894 when a Jewish captain in the French army was framed as a German spy. It was a topic that rumbled on and divided friends and families for the best part of a decade, and Dreyfus's religion was often at the heart of the discussion. 'Anti-Semitism was as French as the croissant,' remarked the historian Eugen Weber, while Léon Blum, a future prime minister and himself Jewish, called the whole affair 'no less violent than the French Revolution'.

Behind the affair was a growing sense of paranoia in Paris, and a certain *fin de siècle* malaise. The Third Republic was still promoting a new, more moral society, but the Church was moving from the public to the private sphere (it was officially separated from the State in France in 1905) – or even out of people's lives entirely. In the world of art, it was felt that nothing was new any more. 'All has been said before us, my dear friend,' declared Gustave Flaubert to Zola. 'We have nothing left but to say the same things, only in a more beautiful form if that is possible.'

Adding to the sense of menace was a series of anarchist bomb attacks in the city, targeting – seemingly at random –

THE FORGOTTEN ARCHITECT OF THE EIFFEL TOWER

Before Gustave Eiffel's tower began its spiky ascent into the Paris skyline, it had already been famously subjected to the insults of a number of artists, writers and architects. 'The useless and monstrous Eiffel Tower', they protested in a letter, was 'the mercenary invention of a machine builder' and a 'gigantic and black factory chimney'.

Eiffel had anticipated such attacks. His team of engineers knew they had the necessary skill to build the tower, the world's largest construction, but he was equally aware that it would lack elegance and grace without the input of an artist. He called once more on his architect friend Stephen Sauvestre, with whom he had worked on the Universal Exhibition of 1878 (for which they had built the gas pavilion).

Sauvestre added a number of features to the basic design of the tower, notably introducing curved arches like skirts between its four feet. In his reply to the doubters, Eiffel emphasized these aesthetic elements. 'The curves of the four edges of the monument . . . will give it a great impression of strength and beauty,' he claimed, and today few people would deny the truth of that.

Eiffel claimed that his tower was 'resounding proof of the progress achieved this century by the art of engineers', but most artists simply refused to believe that engineers could understand anything about beauty. Sauvestre was part of a new generation that would reunite the disciplines of engineering and art. He was one of the first graduates of the École spéciale d'architecture, an institution that was created to bring the world of the École des beaux-arts (where architects had previously trained) into the modern world of iron, steel and concrete.

Beyond his work with Eiffel, Sauvestre was primarily a builder of houses. Many survive in Paris today, most of them in the 17th arrondissement, and are proof of his maxim: no two houses should ever be the same. He was also keen to display on their facades the materials used in the construction of his houses, something that is certainly also true of the Eiffel Tower.

The curves of the Eiffel Tower.

Eugène Atget, *Marchand de vin*, c. 1910.

public transport, cafés and even parliament. With such a loss of bearings, Paris turned to hedonism and became entirely dedicated to the pursuit of pleasure. No one typified this more than the president of the Republic, Félix Faure, who died on 16 February 1899 in the embrace of his mistress Marguerite Steinheil (although, like Marguerite, the real cause of death was quickly covered up).

Such pleasure-seeking and indulgence led Paris to become a city that celebrated itself. This was 'an age when there were ten writers at every dinner party, and each one rushed home to confide the clever or outrageous behaviour of his fellow guests to a journal.' This one-upmanship turned everyone

'Quinquina Dubonnet aperitif dans tous les cafés', advert for Dubonnet, illustrated by Jules Chéret, 1895.

into a writer or actor, but also increased the pressure to perform and raised the likelihood and costs of failure.

The year 1900 arrived with another Universal Exhibition, but this one would be the biggest and best the world had ever seen. It welcomed more than 50 million visitors – more than the entire population of France. Beginning with the

Detail from front page of the newspaper *L'Aurore* from Thursday 13 January 1898 with the letter 'J'accuse . . . !' written by Émile Zola to President Félix Faure accusing the government of anti-Semitism and the unlawful jailing of Alfred Dreyfus.

6-m- (20-ft-) tall sculpture of a woman named *La Parisienne* that dominated the entrance to the exhibition, everything was oversized. At one event, organized for the association of mayors of France, 606 tables were set up for 20,277 elected representatives, and two bottles of wine were allocated to each person.

The exhibition was held at the same time as such monumental changes in society as the arrival of electricity, cars, the telephone, flight, cinema, medical breakthroughs and longer life expectancy. However, in 1900 Paris preferred to show itself off as the world capital of consumerism. The extravagant exhibition left many traces in the city – the Alexandre III bridge, the Grand and Petit Palais – but unfortunately the two-speed moving pavement between the Champ de Mars and Les Invalides did not survive.

The *Parisienne* had been the symbol of the exhibition, and at the beginning of the twentieth century there was a certain flexibility in laws concerning women, although they still earned half as much as men when performing the same jobs. Like that great mascot, women were becoming more visible – and audible – in the city. 'A true Parisienne in 1900', it was noted, 'should not hesitate to give her opinion . . . on a play, a war, a horse, an opera, the marriage of a prince, a strike or some visit of a tsar.'

Ten years later, there was only one topic of conversation for everyone: how to get around the flooded city. At the beginning of 1910 Paris experienced its worst floods for 150 years, and the first to be depicted so graphically on postcards and in photographs. Some 20,000 buildings suffered damage, and it took two months for the waters to drop back to normal levels. The floods severely affected the functioning of the city, but did not prevent Paris from becoming an international leader in industry. By 1913 French factories – particularly those in the Paris region – were manufacturing 45,000 cars a year, making the country the world's largest producer, but it had not invested in defences and war material.

This was a curious oversight in a period when the clouds of war were seemingly building up once again in Europe. In Paris, though, the only battles taking place were at the ballet. In 1913 rioting broke out at the newly opened Théâtre des Champs-Élysées on the opening night of Igor Stravinsky's *The Rite of Spring*, which was judged too avant-garde by more traditional ballet-goers.

By 1914 war appeared imminent, and only the Socialist leader Jean Jaurès was pushing for a peaceful solution in France. On 31 July he spent all day in the Chamber of Deputies pleading with ministers and deputies to show restraint, before having dinner in Le Croissant café, next to the offices of his newspaper, *L'Humanité*. Later that evening, the leader of the German Social Democrats was due in Paris to meet Jaurès and discuss ways of finding a miraculous last-minute framework for peace. When he arrived, he was informed that Jaurès had been assassinated in the café by the aptly named Raoul Villain. Three days later France was at war, something many people had wanted all along. The overwhelming opinion in the country was that expressed by Abel Bonnard, a journalist for the right-wing newspaper *Le Figaro*: 'War refashions everything anew,' he wrote; 'we must embrace it in all its savage poetry.' He can perhaps be forgiven for not imagining just how savage that war would be.

8 Caught on the Battle Lines

As soon as war broke out, Paris was awash with soldiers. Parisians, who had suffered at the hands of the Prussians during the siege of 1870–71 and remembered the triumphant march of Prussian troops down the Champs-Élysées, nurtured a deep-seated resentment against Prussians and Germans, who had also made off with the regions of Alsace and Lorraine. When offered the chance to take revenge on the same foe, many leapt at the opportunity.

Among the hundreds of thousands of young volunteers and conscripts were many well-known personalities. Although Henri Matisse, at 45, was declared too old for service, the painter Raoul Dufy and writer Jean Cocteau became drivers, and the poet Guillaume Apollinaire – who had requested French nationality, despite being of Polish descent, in order to fight – received a head wound early on in the conflict and never really recovered. Even those unable to participate put forward what they could. The scientist Marie Curie offered her medals as precious metal and bought war bonds with the money she had received with her Nobel Prize.

Despite this bluster and bravado, France was ill-equipped for war. The country dreamed of vengeance, but had not invested in the war machine that would help it to achieve its goal. The Germans, on the other hand, had integrated the modern world into their army, in terms of both technology and tactics. At the turn of the century the writer Charles Péguy had noted that 'the world has changed less since Jesus Christ than it has in the last thirty years,' but this did not seem to apply to the French military. Like thousands of other French troops, Péguy would survive barely one month of war, being picked off by a machine-gun bullet in the Battle of the Marne. Such unpreparedness was a strange oversight, since in many other domains the French had made significant advances. As well as succeeding in the mass-production of cars, they were also pioneers in aviation. Frenchmen were the first to cross the Channel (Louis Blériot in 1909) and the Mediterranean (Roland Garros in 1913) by aeroplane. The country had achieved prestige, but had not bothered to develop the air force that might have ended the war quickly.

Paris, the centre of this production and the closest major city to the conflict, was once more the destination for the invading Teutonic forces. Assisted by the Allied Forces, the French kept the Germans at bay, but it quickly became clear that the war had set in for longer than had been first imagined. Amid the fear of imminent invasion, the French capital became a deserted city. Between the young men who had gone to the front line and the middle classes who had escaped to safer parts of France, the population of the city drastically declined. No buses ran, and the Métro operated a reduced timetable, its trains driven for the first time by women. Theatres and cinemas locked their doors; cafés were obliged to close by

Automobiles requisitioned to move troops to the front during the First World War, Paris.

8 pm and restaurants at 9.30 pm. At night, the City of Light was plunged into darkness.

With the rumble of battle audible in the city, Myron Herrick, the American ambassador, reported to his son in a letter that the situation was 'almost beyond human resistance'. He offered to protect Paris's museums under the American flag 'in the custody of humanity at large'. It was an offer that would not be put to the test, but it was an important gesture in Paris from a country that was reluctant to join Europe's conflict. In recognition, Herrick remains the only American ambassador to have a street named after him in Paris.

By August it seemed as though the battle was lost. The French government decamped to Bordeaux, leaving just General Joseph Gallieni – and the spirit of Ste Geneviève, once again – to defend the city. 'Inhabitants of Paris,' the General began solemnly in a dispatch that was quickly pasted on posts, trees and walls around Paris, 'the members of the government have left Paris to give a new impetus to the defence of the nation. I have received a mandate to defend Paris against the invader. This I will fulfil to the end.' The historian – and soldier – Daniel Halévy, who was posted in the city, explained the strange way in which this message gave Parisians hope: 'This soldier's language signified "you will burn, you will die with me, but you will not be delivered." And the people, having read that, left contented.'

Gallieni, who, like Napoléon III, had been captured at the Battle of Sedan in 1870, proved to be an unlikely hero. Before the government left Paris, the 65-year-old veteran, who was suffering from a prostate cancer that would kill him before the end of the war, asked a simple question: 'What do you give me to defend this immense place enclosing the heart and brain of France?' The answer was very little. He was assigned just one unit and the instruction to defend Paris 'à outrance', meaning until death. If the Germans came close, his duty would be to sabotage all bridges in the city, including the pont Neuf, to hold up the invaders. The wily Gallieni, though, sniffed out an opportunity to counter-attack, thrusting at a weak point of a moving German line. To transport troops to that front, taxis were pressed into action, and 60,000 soldiers were sent out of Paris in six hundred red Renault cars, each taking five soldiers at a time, twice a day.

Paris was saved – at least temporarily – and the government returned, as did the thousands of Parisians who had fled at the first sign of danger. 'They all found an apology for their departure,' noted Cocteau, who also observed how quickly the city returned to something close to normal. Venues began putting on concerts again, although Bach, Beethoven and Schubert were dropped from the repertoire.

The war remained very much on the doorstep of Paris, but no longer seemed a looming danger for the city. 'On windless nights', noted the actress and writer Colette, it was possible to hear 'the belch of the howitzers'. From her garden in Paris, one of her friends even danced a tango to the rhythm of the explosions.

Two years after the outbreak of the war, with the first battles having died down and the Germans' push across the country halted, Paris experienced a reasonably quiet period. 'There were two fronts,' Cocteau wrote. 'There was the war front, and then in Paris what might be called the Montparnasse front.' 'We are divided into two foreign countries,' wrote Henri Barbusse in his war novel *Under Fire* (1916). 'The front . . . where there is too much misery, and the rear . . . where there is too much contentment.' Paris had tired of the war and was becoming frivolous once more. Soldiers on leave were surprised to find a city with brightly lit shops, pretty girls, smart cars and little in the way of rationing; the only difficulty for Parisians, it seemed, was how to survive the war without eating croissants. One soldier, Gaston Biron, expressed the bitterness many soldiers felt in a scathing letter to his mother: 'I've noticed, like all my comrades who are left, that these two years of war have, little by little, made the civilian population selfish and indifferent, and that we and the other combatants are almost forgotten.'

In 1918 the war made a comeback in Paris after the German invention of a new, longer-range weapon that was positioned within firing distance of the city. What it boasted in range it

Albert Herter, *Departure of the Infantrymen, August 1914*, 1926, painting at the Gare de l'Est.

A MONUMENTAL PAINTING

The Great War had ended famously with a signature of armistice in a train carriage in the forests of Compiègne, to the north of Paris, but for many it also began in trains, at the city's Gare de l'Est. The significance of this site is celebrated in a painting, *Departure of the Infantrymen, August 1914*, which hangs today in the main hall of the station, although it must now compete with the bright lights of shops and flashing information screens.

The canvas, which has an area of more than 60 sq. m (645 sq. ft), is the work of the American artist Albert Herter. In 1926 he presented it to the company that ran the station, but it was more than just a generous gift. Herter had lost a son in the conflict, and the painting is a monumental tribute to his memory. Executed in soft, melancholic blues, greys and browns, it describes a scene that would have been typical during the war.

The painting is built around a trinity of the father, the mother and the departing, soon to be dearly departed, son, who is catching a train to the front. Both parents seem already to be in mourning, and more elderly than they would have been when waving off their son; the father carries a bouquet of flowers, hand upon heart, and the mother clasps her hands.

It is the son, Everit, however, who is the focus of the composition. At first glance he seems triumphant and unconcerned, with his arms held aloft while people at his feet weep and embrace. A closer look reveals the flowers sticking out of his rifle, his thrown-back head and his arms, which clearly form a cross. Everit here is a Christ-like, sacrificial figure.

Everit Herter, like his father and mother before him, had chosen an artistic path, and had studied to be a painter. His father had spent several years in France, which perhaps explains why Everit signed up with the French army. Tragically, Everit was killed only months before the Armistice, becoming another member of the wasted generation.

Victory Day celebration, 14 July 1919, Arc de Triomphe.

lost in accuracy; all the shells were aimed at the Louvre, but instead they landed in random parts of the city. On Good Friday in March, though, 75 people were killed when a shell struck the church of Saint-Gervais, causing part of the roof to collapse during a service.

Paris survived this second onslaught, too. By the autumn the war was over, and the Armistice was signed in a railway carriage in Compiègne on 11 November. Despite being so close to the heart of the battle, Paris suffered, as the historian Graham Robb has remarked, 'little more than a chipped turret and a dented portcullis': only 266 people were killed in the city during the war from zeppelin raids and shelling. Immediately after the war, at least that many would die each day of Spanish influenza (30,000 victims were counted in the Paris region during the pandemic of 1918).

For a year from January 1919, Paris hosted the Peace Conference, a series of discussions that were supposed to be about crippling the German war machine but which were actually more about humiliating Germany and sharing out the spoils among the winners. With 27 Allied countries involved in the negotiations and housed in the best hotels, Parisians rapidly grew tired of the huge delegations, which were using up scarce resources. With enormous differences of opinion among the Allies, it looked as though a deal would be impossible and the war would need to be fought again. France, though, was leading the negotiations, and – keen to avoid any more suffering in the country (France had lost 1.4 million people, 7 per cent of its total population) – forced through a treaty by the deadline. It was eventually signed on 28 June 1919 in the Galerie des Glaces at Versailles, where Wilhelm had crowned himself emperor in 1871. For the French, both the signature and its location signified the circle completed, but the terms were so severe that it instead represented only half a circle and a virtual guarantee of future conflict.

The war had decimated France, but in 1921 the population of Paris reached 2.9 million, an all-time high. Growth in Paris, though, was dwarfed by the expansion of the city's suburbs. Between 1850 and 1940 the Paris region absorbed nine-tenths of the country's population increase, and between 1914 and 1942 some 92 per cent of new houses built in the region were in the suburbs – most with a stunning lack of planning and infrastructure.

In Paris itself, everything was far more chic. The city was far from being wealthy in the 1920s, but it produced a golden age of creation, celebrated most notably at the International Exhibition of Modern Decorative and Industrial Arts in 1925. Combining a post-war desire to party with a dose of the newly formed school of Surrealism, Paris became the beating heart of the *années folles* (the roaring twenties). It also became an immensely attractive place for Americans. In 1927 some 15,000 Americans were living in Paris, mostly on the Left Bank. They came for two reasons: a small allowance in dollars went a long

Salvador Dalí and Man Ray hamming it up.

way in Paris; and the city was a place where – as Henry Miller declared – 'all boundaries fade away.' Some came to enjoy the fête; others, including Ernest Hemingway, Gertrude Stein, Dorothy Parker and F. Scott Fitzgerald, also came to write.

For black Americans, many of whom had come to France during the First World War, Paris provided a great opportunity to find a position in society and express themselves artistically. Many had stayed in the city after the First World War, enamoured of the freedom they found there. It was something Josephine Baker certainly appreciated, and she could often be seen walking her pet leopard, Chiquita, down the Champs-Élysées.

There were not only Americans in the city; to spend time in Paris was obligatory for artists, no matter where they later wanted to set themselves up: 'Any obscure poet, any painter who wanted to succeed in Bucharest or Seville, must necessarily . . . have done a little military service at la Rotonde or at la Coupole.' These two cafés in Montparnasse were the new centre of the art scene, which had moved from Montmartre, now a 'ville morte, à la manière de Venise' (a dead city, in the style of Venice) thanks to tourism and the rising cost of living.

Paris in the 1920s may have been the scene of an international festival of dancing, painting and writing, but it was not much fun for the majority of Parisians, as George Orwell described in *Down and Out in Paris and London* (1933): 'There was a girl in a bistro near my hotel who worked from seven in the morning till midnight for a whole year, only sitting down to her meals. I remember once asking her to come to a dance, and she laughed and said that she had not been further than the street corner for several months. She was consumptive, and died about the time I left Paris.' And yet, in a thoroughly Monty Pythonesque manner, she could be described as being

Gertrude Stein in her Paris studio, 1930.

one of the lucky ones. Orwell encountered many others, without work, who did not eat for days on end and who had not changed their clothes for months.

The stock market crash in 1929 sent the Americans back home or elsewhere, but the ripples hit Paris a year or so later, launching the beginning of a very dark decade in its history. Indeed, added to the five years of war at the end of the decade, and then a further five years of recovery, this period represented possibly the worst twenty years in the city's existence.

With the rise of Adolf Hitler, neighbouring Germany was clearly becoming menacing again, but alongside the challenging economic conditions, French politics was in a catastrophic state. There were five governments in eighteen months mid-decade, all with the same faces, a situation that encouraged a move towards the extreme right, and even the assassination of a president, Paul Doumer, in 1932. On 6 February 1934 some 40,000 sympathizers of these parties marched to the French parliament. A battle with the police on the pont de la Concorde left sixteen dead and 650 injured, and brought down yet another government.

Left-wing parties finally decided to unite their forces as the Front Populaire, and won the election in May 1936. Léon Blum formed a government that soon voted in sweeping and radical reform, including paid holidays, a forty-hour week, wage increases and wider representation for workers. This being France, though, the workers were still not happy and went on strike, eventually bringing down the Blum government.

The brief utopia had not satisfied the workers' demands, and was also a luxury that France could ill afford. Blum, though, was unrepentant: 'I had the feeling, in spite of everything, of having brought a lull, a vista, into their dark, difficult lives . . . we had given them hope.'

The year 1939 marked the 150th anniversary of the French Revolution, but nobody was in a mood to celebrate – with

Josephine Baker playing clarinet at the Caf' Conc Festival, Montrouge, Paris, 1926.

good reason. On 3 September France was once more at war with Germany. Paris, always a target for the Germans, felt in imminent danger, convinced that the enemy again possessed a far superior war machine. But for the first eight months of the conflict, Paris enjoyed the *drôle de guerre* (phoney war), in which little appeared to be happening across Europe. The weather in the spring of 1940 was excellent, and the Parisians relaxed at race meetings, in cafés and at the theatre. Yet by May the Germans had pushed through the Netherlands and Belgium and had broken into France. The acclaimed Maginot Line of defences on the French border had not held – or had simply been bypassed. In Paris, people dusted down the sarcophagus of Ste Geneviève once again and paraded the golden casket through the city. The government hesitated about leaving the city, and then decided that it had to stay this time. It was a decision not shared by two-thirds of the city's residents, though, who began a mass exodus towards safer regions of the country.

Exodus from Paris, June 1940.

The city was bombed for the first time in June 1940, and 250 civilians were killed, almost as many as had been killed in Paris during the entire First World War. Cannon fire could be heard constantly, and the city was to all intents and purposes under siege by the Germans for the third time in seventy years. Eventually, on 10 June, the government, including General Charles de Gaulle, did leave Paris, and the following day it was declared an open city. Paris had given up without a fight, a possibly surprising decision but one that saved the city from much damage. For most across France, it meant the end of the conflict. 'France deprived of Paris would become a body without a head. The war had been lost,' declared the essayist André Maurois.

Under Lieutenant Colonel Dr Hans Speidel and the 87th infantry, the German occupiers arrived in Paris on 14 June, and immediately took possession of the Hôtel de Ville and Les Invalides. A week later France signed a humiliating armistice in Compiègne, in exactly the same train carriage that had been used in 1918. The next day, Sunday 23 June, Hitler visited Paris for the first and only time, accompanied by the architect Albert Speer and the artist Arno Breker.

Hitler came to observe the conquered jewel, but also, more mundanely, to fulfil one of his old art-student wishes. 'Like you,' he said to Breker, 'I would have studied here if fate had not driven me into politics, for my aspirations before the First World War were entirely artistic.' The small group arrived at about 6 am and rushed round the city, taking in the Opéra ('the most beautiful theatre in the world'), the Trocadéro (where they posed for a photo with the Eiffel Tower as backdrop, to 'prove to the world that Adolf Hitler had been to Paris'), Napoléon's tomb at Les Invalides (the high point of the tour), the Panthéon (with its 'wretched coldness') and Sacré-Coeur ('appalling').

The whole tour took about three hours, and Hitler – on his unique trip to Paris – met barely a single Parisian. He had imagined Paris to be somehow grander, but was reassured that Berlin would easily become the new centre of world civilization. 'When we are finished with Berlin, Paris will be nothing but a shadow, so why should we destroy it?' he told Breker afterwards.

Many of those who had left the city at the end of May returned a few months later, often under pressure from the Germans. Cinemas and theatres reopened, and people carried on with life almost as normal, mostly choosing to ignore the smartly dressed soldiers around them. 'I am pleased with the Parisians,' the writer Jean Guéhenno noted in his diary in 1940. 'They cross paths with the Germans as they would cross paths with dogs and cats. It seems they neither see them nor hear them.' For others, there were tiny acts of resistance. To mark the first anniversary of the German invasion of Paris, one girl went to school with a black ribbon in her hair. 'Who are you in mourning for?' asked the headmistress. Without hesitating, the young pupil replied, 'For Paris.' She was sent home for eight days.

Adopting the status of a minor city suited many people, including Colette, who admitted that she 'liked spending her wars in Paris', since the city was 'the only village where one can possibly live during a war'. She spent much of the war running her beauty parlour in the rue Saint-Honoré or in her cosy apartment in the Palais-Royal, practising 'le sage repliement sur soi' – or, very roughly translated, lying low. Colette had better reason than many to be discreet: her husband was Jewish. He was forced to wear the yellow star and was briefly arrested, but wrangling in the background soon resulted in his release. The couple were even later invited for tea by the German ambassador's wife, who was a fan of Colette's work.

Most artists justified their continued passive collaboration by pointing out that any curb on social life would affect Parisians more than it would their German occupiers. They chose to carry on working and performing and to ignore the Germans, but they also had to ignore signs in theatres that read 'no dogs or Jews'.

In March 1942 *rafles* (round-ups) and deportations began in Paris, and the French police showed excessive zeal by also taking children and babies, something that was not in their original remit. Whole communities were held first in an indoor cycling arena – with little water or sanitation – or a recently built suburban estate, before being sent by train to the camps. In 1940 Paris counted a population of around 150,000 Jewish people; by the end of the war, that figure had dropped to about 50,000.

The German invasion of Russia in June 1941 ended the pact between the two countries, and also freed the Paris Communists from neutrality. Many formed resistance movements, fighting underground battles against the occupiers and the *Milice* – the hated French military police – who had taken over the old French Communist Party headquarters in Paris. For long months Paris was an irrelevant sideshow in the war, but in April 1944 Allied Forces began bombing key positions in the city. An air raid

Liberation, 25 August 1944: Allied tanks and half-tracks pass through the Arc de Triomphe.

around Montmartre killed hundreds and brought Marshal Philippe Pétain to Paris for the first time since the occupation, just short of his 88th birthday. Paris was suffering, but also took the bombs as a sign of approaching liberation.

Following the D-Day landings in June and the Allied sweep across northwest France, the great race to liberate Paris and save the city from destruction was on. It became a race between French troops (led by generals de Gaulle and Jacques-Philippe Leclerc) and the Americans (led by General George Patton), who had at first wanted to chase the Germans rapidly out of the country and bypass Paris altogether. In Paris itself, groups of Resistance fighters under Colonel Henri Rol-Tanguy did not want to wait to be liberated, and began their own uprising on 13 August. It was a critical time for Paris: Hitler asked the city commander, Dietrich von Choltitz, 'Is Paris burning?', and Raoul Nordling, the Swedish consul general in Paris, negotiated with von Choltitz to protect prisoners and prevent the destruction of the city.

General de Gaulle had another reason to race to Paris. 'Go fast,' he told Leclerc; 'we cannot have another Commune.' His greatest fear was that Communist Party sympathizers would fill the void left by retreating German troops. Leclerc did eventually arrive first and in time. The next day, 26 August, was de Gaulle's moment. Ignoring the sporadic fighting that was still taking place in the city, he marched triumphantly down the Champs-Élysées, and then on to the Hôtel de Ville, where he made one of his landmark speeches. 'Paris outragé, Paris brisé, Paris martyrisé, mais Paris libérté' (An outraged Paris! A broken Paris! A martyred Paris! But a liberated Paris!) he called out to the mesmerized crowd below – and to audiences across the world.

'The end of German occupation has liberated my camera!' the photographer Jacques-Henri Lartigue, who had kept one roll of film aside throughout the conflict specifically to capture the liberation of Paris, proclaimed with joy. After his excitement came relief: 'The miracle is not that she is only scarred nor that she has not been completely demolished, but that she is still here.' Paris had somehow managed to come through the world's two deadliest conflicts with her beauty intact.

9 1968 and All That

Charles de Gaulle was undoubtedly one of the winners of the Second World War, but within a year of the conflict ending he had stepped out of the limelight. A military leader, he quickly tired of the post-war political wrangling, which he called 'an absurd ballet', and slipped away to semi-retirement, declaring enigmatically, 'J'attends' (I'll wait). He would bide his time, confident that the country would soon come crawling back to him.

Paris had been liberated in 1944, but the purges and punishment of those who had collaborated with the German occupiers, a process known as the *épuration*, continued for several years afterwards. First came the *épuration sauvage*, spontaneous lynchings and humiliations that included shaving the heads of women who were said to have been 'horizontal collaborators' for having relationships with German soldiers.

Among those women was Arletty, a popular singer and actress who had spent much of the war in Paris with Hans Jürgen Soehring, ten years her junior and an officer of the Luftwaffe. In her defence, she allegedly declared: 'My heart is French but my arse is international.' Later, put under house arrest – comfortably for eighteen months in the Château de la Houssaye near Paris – she was given a stern telling-off and her freedom back and was quickly able to resume her career.

Others were dealt with more severely. The *épuration* of the administration, police, magistrates, politicians and press – 60,000 trials in all – was an administrative and legal nightmare that was almost impossible to keep up with. From 1945 until 1949 these *épurations* became a series of show trials, made all the more tense by the return of emaciated survivors from the

Arletty in *Les Enfants du paradis* (dir. Marcel Carné, 1945).

camps. Following these trials, 767 people were executed; that number does not include the country's wartime leader, Pétain, who was declared too old for the guillotine. He had refused to defend himself, and was exiled to a prison on the remote island of Yeu off the western coast of France, where he eventually died in 1951 aged 95.

If France was still fighting an internal post-war battle, it was at least – finally – working on lasting peace with Germany. In 1950 the European Coal and Steel Community was created in Paris, following a proposition by the French foreign minister, Robert Schuman. Bringing together the European 'six' (France, West Germany, Italy, the Netherlands, Belgium and Luxembourg), it was a forerunner of the European Economic Community. The United Kingdom had not been invited to join this club, but was an important member of the military organization NATO, which was created in 1948, also in Paris, to counter the new Soviet bloc.

Post-war reconstruction was under way, but there was much to do in Paris and in France. Infrastructure across the country had been demolished during the war, and housing in the capital was in a piteous state – not because of war damage, but simply because it was all very dilapidated. 'In the city ocean, insalubrious slums emerge like rocks of grime,' wrote the poet Jacques Audiberti of mid-century Paris. At the beginning of the 1950s, half of all housing in the city had no bathroom or toilet, and many apartments had no running water. It was no surprise that tuberculosis was still killing thousands in poorer districts. The crumbling of this deteriorating city was reflected in the dismantling of the French empire. Post-war uprisings across the globe – an offshoot of the new Cold War – cost France many of its colonies. In 1954 it abandoned its eastern territories during the Indo-Chinese War, but it was almost immediately engulfed in an extremely bloody conflict in Algeria.

The year ended with the coldest winter in living memory, and dozens of homeless and poorly housed people, including several children, succumbed to the freeze. The situation finally forced Parisian leaders to accept that the city had a severe problem with housing and the poor, especially when a media-friendly priest known as Abbé Pierre launched an appeal for aid. Forced through public pressure to do something, the country's regional authorities began building, but almost exclusively high-rise blocks in the suburbs, where quantity was more important than quality.

Paris remained fundamentally unchanged, although certain sociologists believe that its poor-quality housing did at least provide the catalyst for productive new subcultures. People who did not want to stay in their tiny, damp, unheated apartments spent as much time as possible in the city's cafés and jazz clubs. In the 1950s such comforts were easily found in the district of Saint-Germain-des-Près, which became the existential heart of the city. During this golden age, this tiny district and its inhabitants were behind all new movements in literature, theatre, cinema, music and, above all, philosophy. 'Saint-Germain-des-Près is an island,' wrote Boris Vian, one of its citizen observers. Its territory could be mapped by the numerous drinking establishments – Café Flore and Les Deux Magots, Brasserie Lipp and Le Tabou – and its natives easily identified by their dress, mainly black polo necks.

From left to right: Jean-Paul Sartre, Boris and Michelle Vian and Simone de Beauvoir in Saint-Germain-des-Près, 1949.

Simone de Beauvoir and Jean-Paul Sartre were the queen and king, Albert Camus and Man Ray the princes, and the singer Juliette Gréco the enchanting princess.

If Saint-Germain-des-Près had glamour (which would end by killing off its remaining bohemian credentials), much of the rest of Paris in the 1950s was simply grimy and gritty. The historian and Paris explorer Eric Hazan remembers a Marais 'black with dirt and soot, the courtyards cluttered with outhouses covered with corrugated iron'. Not far from there, Beaubourg – where the Centre Pompidou stands today – was 'a cobbled void that served as a garage at night for the market trucks of Les Halles and as a shelter for hasty and paid-for embraces.'

In 1962 André Malraux, the country's minister of culture, brought in new legislation to clean up the city. 'Old' Paris, particularly the Marais, was accorded protection and given a thorough scrubbing-down. This changed the colour of the city, turning it from black back to light grey and cream, but this toilette also led indirectly to today's fossilization. The old working-class units of Hazan's youth were transformed into trendy boutiques, and the Marais into a district that he now calls a 'Disneyland for cultured tourists'.

Before this sprucing-up, the begrimed and dishevelled city reflected the country's political situation. The Fourth Republic put in place after the Second World War was a failure. Faced with the impossibility of forming any kind of lasting government, the country turned to Charles de Gaulle – as he had always known it would. He returned in 1958, and quickly organized a referendum to create a new Fifth Republic (which still holds today), based on a monarchical president

The terrace of the Café de Flore.

with vastly increased powers. Sartre quipped that de Gaulle wanted to be 'King Charles XI', and declared that, although an atheist, he would rather vote for God, because 'he is more modest'. France – and the rest of the world – would soon become familiar with this new era of defiant *Gaullisme*.

If the political situation was finally more settled, the continued conflict in Algeria was still causing immense problems, and Paris was on the front line. On one side were the Algerians who lived in the city, some connected to radical groups (such as the Front de Libération Nationale, or FLN; the National Liberation Front), some simply protesting against the curfews imposed on them. On the other side, a second faction made up of disgruntled paramilitary groups waged a campaign of terror in the city to ensure that France stayed in Algeria. On one single night this group, the Organisation de l'armée secrète (OAS; the Secret Army Organisation), set off eighteen incendiary devices across Paris. The tension crackling in the air led to tragedy in October 1961, when an anti-curfew demonstration in Paris was put down violently by the city police, itself the recent victim of numerous assassinations. Exactly what happened has never been established clearly, but estimates today put at about one hundred the number of Algerian protesters who were killed. A plaque was unveiled forty years later on the pont Saint-Michel, near the place where most victims were believed to have been thrown into the river. It was the first official recognition of the massacre, but, placed at ankle height, the message remains almost invisible.

The Évian Accords in March 1962 brought to an end the war in Algeria, but not the reverberations in Paris. In August President de Gaulle avoided assassination by centimetres when a ragtag crowd of soldiers and mercenaries fired on the presidential cavalcade as it passed through the quiet suburb of Clamart. The OAS ringleader, Colonel Jean-Marie Bastien-Thiry, was caught and became the first French officer in decades to be killed by firing squad. Meanwhile de Gaulle, having survived five assassination attempts at the beginning of the 1960s, perhaps felt himself to be invincible. The country, ever more wealthy, also reflected his confidence. In 1965, with France now boasting its own nuclear capability, de Gaulle pulled the country out of NATO – and, as a result, NATO from Paris. It was another example of the president's hot streak of independence: he also recognized Mao's Peking regime in 1964 and became the first Western head of government to visit Khrushchev's Soviet Union.

De Gaulle was a leading world statesman, but the general and his wife, Yvonne, were ill at ease in international Paris, and were almost never seen eating in the chic restaurants or at cultural events. If the couple preferred life at their country house in the east of France, de Gaulle nevertheless believed that Paris should reflect the 'grandeur' of France. For the president, this principally meant new infrastructure (La Défense business district, the Périphérique ring road, rapid transportation systems), but little in the way of spectacular architecture.

De Gaulle was re-elected president in 1965, but his relationship with the French was souring, and he received a much-reduced majority that necessitated a second round of voting. It was not that France was suffering – the country was wealthy and growing rapidly – but rather that it was becoming a little dull, particularly for a new generation looking for a little more *liberté*. It was also distinctly patriarchal. It was not until 1965 that women were finally allowed to open their own bank accounts without the permission of a father or husband.

An uprising occurred in May 1968, during which one of the first signs to be seen was 'La France s'ennuie' (France is bored), a slogan that had been seen in 1848 at the end of the monarchy. Alongside it was another, declaring 'de Gaulle aux archives' (de Gaulle to the archives). The year 1968 was the tenth anniversary of de Gaulle's return to power, and for some, the time was starting to feel long. Across the world, protests were staged against the war in Vietnam, against the Soviet crushing of the Prague Spring, and for civil rights in America. The uprising of May 1968 in Paris was equally iconic, although the people's demands were far

May 1968: students hurl paving stones at police in the rue Saint-Jacques in Paris's Latin Quarter during the student riots. Police reply with tear gas.

less clear. The sociologist Edgar Morin has described it as both 'gigantic and miniscule', immense in its influence, tiny in its organization. For Eric Hazan, a publisher and Left Bank figure at the time, 'it unfolded in the style of a programmed defeat', but any concept of an eventual victory seemed almost irrelevant anyway.

The protest began in the dreary suburb of Nanterre, where a university had been built between *bidonville* shanty towns and roaring aerial motorways. The complaints were prosaic ones about food, poor-quality infrastructure, lack of teaching staff and foggy future perspectives. In an era of free love, the fact that men and women had separate residences, locked up each night at 10, also rankled. 'They can see each other in the amphitheatres,' declared de Gaulle. His minister of sport, in Nanterre to open a new swimming pool, told protesters who had asked why the government refused to discuss contraception, 'You'd be better off diving three times into the pool.'

Leaking out of Nanterre to the Sorbonne and other places of learning, May 1968 was essentially a form of consumer protest. The students were rising up against universities that had become bloated knowledge factories manned by robot professors. With the number of students in France having increased from 240,000 in 1960 to around 600,000 by 1968, it also represented the snapping of institutions that had pulled the elastic too tight. For many protesters, though, the period was above all one of riotous fun, an obscure struggle played out to a rock-and-roll soundtrack. 'Lennon played a more important role than Lenin,' noted the journalist Laurent Joffrin. Perhaps the undeclared final goal was simply to destroy the old regime and stuffy, conservative, bourgeois Paris. 'Ici bientôt, de charmantes ruines' (Here soon, charming ruins), read one piece of graffiti on a historic Left Bank building.

Young, media-friendly and articulate, the protesters possessed a glamour that made the uprising seem all the more alluring. 'In the short and long terms, they enhanced the attraction of the Latin Quarter as a tourist destination,' pointed out the historian Graham Robb; 'May 68 was a revolution with its own theme park.' Sightseers and tourists were seen taking early 'selfies' on the barricades, and shops in the area sold Che Guevara T-shirts and other revolutionary paraphernalia from the very beginning of the uprising.

Curiously, the protests in Paris took place just as the city was hosting Vietnam peace talks. Representatives of South Vietnam were staying in Hôtel Claridge on the Champs-Élysées, and those from North Vietnam in the Lutetia on the Left Bank; negotiations were held at the Hôtel Majestic. Shuttled back and forth between the hotels, the teams attempting to end a conflict thousands of miles away were held up by roadblocks, regularly tasted tear gas and were surrounded by the constant hum of demonstrations.

The protests spread outwards from the academic world to become a more general conflict, and by the end of the month ten million people had downed tools. The Communist Party had never given the movement its support, choosing instead to portray the protesters as rich kids fighting to preserve their privileges. In reality, the movement was a threat to the Communist Party itself, and a reminder of collaborations of workers and intellectuals that had brought down regimes in Paris in 1830 and 1848.

At the height of the uprising, France was asking itself one question: where was Charles de Gaulle? The president had indeed left Paris, but was negotiating the support of the army in case the situation worsened. Comforted with this military backing, he returned with another of his landmark interventions. He chose to speak on the radio, because he knew the effect his voice still had on the population, but was also aware that his ageing physique was not an advantage in the new age of television. This proved a political masterstroke, and one million people marched in support on the Champs-Élysées that same evening. A month later de Gaulle's ruling party won 358 out of 485 seats in parliamentary elections, the biggest majority since the Second Empire.

The president had transformed May 1968 into a much less radical June 1968, but despite the election victory, the magic of de Gaulle's 'reign' had been lost. A year later he resigned after losing a minor referendum vote. A further year later he was dead. Having never been a great lover of Paris, he insisted on being kept away from the Panthéon – traditional resting place of the country's great men – and was instead buried near his country house.

De Gaulle's largely apolitical prime minister, Georges Pompidou, took over the running of the country. Pompidou might have been more of a banker than a statesman, but he was also a resolute modernist, particularly when it came to art and architecture. He was a great lover of Paris, too, although he felt the city must change. 'Paris must adapt itself to the auto-mobile,' he declared, and the simple statistics seemed to back him up. The number of cars in the city had doubled, from one million in 1960 to two million by the end of the decade.

For the first time in decades, Paris began to change visually, mostly by growing upwards. Tallest of all was the Montparnasse

The Olympiades: when a window in Paris planning rules allowed the construction of tower blocks.

Tower, but entire new districts of tower blocks sprang up alongside the Eiffel Tower, at the place d'Italie and at the periphery of the city. For Pompidou, such projects reflected an international capital approaching the twenty-first century. He could not help noticing that in comparison, ancient Paris was starting to look rather Lilliputian. 'I know I shouldn't say this,' he declared, 'but the towers of Notre-Dame . . . they're too short.'

In 1974 Pompidou became the first president to die in office since Paul Doumer was assassinated in 1932, and the first to fall victim to an illness. Following him in power was the much younger Valéry Giscard d'Estaing, who was nevertheless much more classical in his tastes. 'The age of giant cities and over-large organizations is over,' he said, after bringing in laws to protect historic Paris. The city had in any case been forced to downsize. Giscard d'Estaing's arrival coincided with an international financial crisis, and for France, the end of the *Trente glorieuses*, thirty consecutive years of growth in the economy and the population. Paris lost half a million people to emigration, primarily from the working class, which was suffering most in the downturn.

Ernest Pignon-Ernest, *Les Expulsés*, 1977, silkscreen prints: a portrait of
eviction.

THE WRITING ON THE WALL

In 1971, a century after the *Semaine sanglante* that brought to a bloody end the revolutionary government of the Paris Commune, the artist Ernest Pignon-Ernest wanted to produce something that would suitably mark the anniversary. 'It wasn't possible for me to summarize such an event on a canvas,' he declared. 'I had to demonstrate on the ground and return to the places that were steeped in history.' Thus was born the urban art movement in Paris.

Pignon-Ernest chose to reproduce dozens of life-size photos of slaughtered Communards and place them in significant locations, such as on the steps of the Sacré-Coeur, a monument built in 'atonement' for the sins of the Commune. For other pioneering artists, including Jacques Villeglé and Gérard Zlotykamien, this act of creating in specific, symbolic places became a leitmotif.

Such ephemeral creations – perhaps a natural extension of the street protests and slogans of May 1968 – also examined nuclear conflict, abortion and forced eviction. The street became the natural habitat of these artists, who had nothing to sell but ideas, and whose goal was to give Parisians an electric shock, forcing these topics into the everyday environment.

All three artists are still active today, but the urban art movement has slowly become synonymous with street art, which privileges the quality of a surface over the symbolism of a work. This evolution began in the more nihilistic 1980s, when a new generation of Paris artists, including Blek le Rat (a major influence on today's superstar Banksy), Jérôme Mesnager, Jef Aérosol and Miss.Tic began using the city as a canvas – and making a living from their art.

Although today's artists draw energy from certain locations, such as the now underground route of the Bièvre river or the post-industrial landscapes of northeast Paris, the movement is now less about protest and more about decoration and self-promotion. Cleaned up, much of the art is tacitly supported by the city of Paris and even something of a tourist attraction.

President François Mitterrand posing in front of the Louvre Pyramid on 29 March 1989, the day of his inauguration.

Paris had at least reclaimed its independence, with the return of an elected mayor. Following this first vote for more than a hundred years, the future president, Jacques Chirac, took office in the Hôtel de Ville in March 1976. 'I have come to the capital of France because, in our history, since the Revolution in 1789, each time Paris has fallen, France has been defeated,' he declared. Chirac would stay for eighteen years, winning again – more convincingly still – in 1983 and 1989.

Paris stood firmly to the right of the political spectrum, but France as a whole turned left in 1981, when the serial Socialist candidate François Mitterrand was finally elected president. With the new president came the return of monumental *grands projets* for Paris, designed in part to ensure the glory and immortality of someone who became known as the 'pharaoh'. (This, though, was also Mitterrand's own myth-making. An amateur of the occult, it was said that he believed himself to be the reincarnation of Seti I.)

Nine large-scale building projects were selected to transform the city, some of which were already on the drawing board before Mitterrand's arrival. Most were controversial, partly because people questioned whether it was wise to spend so much money on the capital of a country that was looking to decentralize, and partly because of inevitable questions of taste. If Carlos Ott's graceless Opéra Bastille building was, in the architect's own words, 'a functional project that is not essentially aesthetic', the opposite was true of I. M. Pei's pyramid at the Louvre. Yet, in common with other once-controversial projects in the city, the pyramid has become a recognized icon.

Former mayor Chirac moved across the city to become president of the Republic on 7 May 1995, the day before the

Scene from Mathieu Kassovitz's film *La Haine* (1995), 'a story about a society falling'.

country celebrated the fiftieth anniversary of the end of the Second World War. But at the beginning of his mandate, it almost seemed as though France were still at war. Between July and October 1995 France suffered eleven terrorist attacks, seven of them in Paris. The following year an attack on the RER transport system at Port-Royal station killed four people. The wave of attacks was attributed to Algerian separatists, but no one was ever prosecuted.

The tension and paranoia in the city and its suburbs – where the transport bombs had been planted – were captured in Mathieu Kassovitz's powerful film *La Haine* (1995), which was nominated for the Palme d'Or at the Cannes Film Festival. The brooding black-and-white tale of a group of young men from the Paris suburbs ends with a tragic police blunder, the almost inevitably violent result of mutual distrust and animosity. To quote the last lines of the film, it was 'a story about a society falling. On the way down it keeps telling itself "So far so good, so far so good, so far so good." How you fall doesn't matter. It's how you land.'

By the end of the century it seemed that Paris, like a twisting cat, might just land on its feet – and this thanks to a sporting event. The 1998 FIFA World Cup, held in France, had for a centrepiece the new – and imaginatively named – Stade de France, built on the site of an old Gaz de France coking plant in the once royal but more recently deprived suburb of Saint-Denis.

France won the final at the stadium, beating Brazil 3-0 thanks largely to national icon (and son of Algerian immigrants) Zinédine Zidane. Hundreds of thousands of people headed straight for the Champs-Élysées, the scene of all national celebrations, where the message 'black-blanc-beur' (black-white-Arab) was projected on to the Arc de Triomphe. It seemed that the team, several members of which had been brought up in the Paris suburbs, reflected the country's new identity. As the demographer Michèle Tribalat, an immigration specialist, pointed out, the team had 'done more for integration than years of urban politics'. It was at least a comforting thought to take into the twenty-first century.

10 Expansion or Preservation?

In 1860 Jules Verne wrote a novel imagining how Paris would look exactly a hundred years later. There would be Métro trains running on compressed air, hydrogen-driven cars, skyscraping hotels housing 20,000 people and a giant port with a 150-m (500-ft) lighthouse. Reflecting on a dystopian world in which science has killed art, Michel Dufrénoy, the hero of the story, looks down sadly from the Père Lachaise cemetery on Paris 'and its one hundred thousand tightly-packed houses, between which rise up the flocculent chimneys of ten thousand factories.'

The novel, *Paris in the Twentieth Century*, was not published in Verne's lifetime. In fact, it wasn't until the 1990s that the author's prescient descriptions of fax machines, telephones and even the electric chair were revealed to the world. What Verne had not imagined, though, was just how similar the city would be a hundred years later – and still again fifty years after that. As he was writing, Paris was transforming itself into one of the world's most modern cities. Since then, it has struggled to project itself into the future, preferring instead to keep a comfortable foot in the past.

This taste for nostalgia was reflected in one of the highest-grossing French films of the beginning of the twenty-first century, *Le Fabuleux destin d'Amélie Poulain* (2001; released in English as *Amélie*). Its director, Jean-Pierre Jeunet, painted Paris as a charming, animated postcard, a pretty and benevolent place that was impossible to date. The film struck gold across the world by chiming with many people's vision of the city: romantic, colourful, enticing and, above all, ageless.

Exactly a month before the film was released Paris did something it had never done before: on 25 March 2001 it elected a Socialist mayor. Although the new man – Bertrand Delanoë – was only the city's thirteenth mayor in its two-thousand-year history, it still represented a step change for Paris. The city may have been the scene of regular rebellion and revolt, but politically it had always been conservative. It still looked much the same as it had a hundred years earlier, but something was changing. Paris was still Paris, but the Parisian was evolving. In place of the stereotypical untrustworthy, quarrelsome merchant, the twenty-first-century Parisian was well off, certainly, but with a social conscience. In other words, a BoBo, a 'bourgeois bohemian'.

The French definition of this American term was more akin to the Champagne Socialist – a description that certainly seemed to fit Delanoë. The academic Philippe Subra has argued that the Paris BoBo simply represents 'the most visible incarnation of tendencies that are becoming progressively pre-eminent among the middle classes as a whole', but it did nevertheless seem that the city had turned over a new page. Instead of landmark architectural projects and a push towards the creation of wealth, there was greater interest in the environment, greater tolerance of differences in sexuality and origin, and new modes of consumption and socializing.

It was a modification of Parisian society that the parties on the right had not foreseen. That said, it was not simply a change in the demographics and mood of Paris that pushed them out of office, but the numerous financial and political scandals they had got themselves mixed up in. Just before the election in 2001, the sitting mayor, Jean Tiberi, was implicated in a scheme whereby eight hundred voters were added to the electoral list in a close-fought district where they didn't actually live, in exchange for social housing, places in city crèches or even jobs.

The first mandate of the Socialists confirmed the city's new zeitgeist. Within a year of the election, car drivers began to see what they believed to be their boulevards eaten up by bus and cycle lanes, and the city welcomed the first of a series of spectacular (and much copied) happenings. There was Paris-Plage, in which imported sand, palm trees and deck-chairs were laid out alongside the Seine (although the sun, unfortunately, was not guaranteed), and the Nuit Blanche, an all-night circuit taking art to unexpected locations.

The election of Delanoë was revolutionary for another reason: it was the first time that one of the world's major cities had elected an openly homosexual mayor, and it underlined once more the city's reputation for tolerance and openness. Equally of interest in Paris was the constitution of the first Executive Committee under the new mayor. Of the 33 deputies, eighteen were female, the first time women had ever been in a majority on the city council. This positive new direction for Paris was confirmed when in 2014, after Delanoë's second mandate, his deputy, Anne Hidalgo, was elected the city's first female mayor.

If at the beginning of the century Paris was run by a new team with a new mantra, it still seemed unsure of its place in the world. There was a feeling that it was declining in influence and attractiveness compared to the new global metropolises as well as to old rivals. In July 2005 this was apparently confirmed when London was surprisingly chosen over the French capital to host the 2012 Olympics. That day I was standing alongside thousands of Parisians in front of a giant screen at the Hôtel de Ville, fully expecting – as were all the other people there – to see 'Paris' pulled out of the envelope. When 'London' appeared, an immense weight of silence suddenly dropped on the city. I quickly slunk away before anyone realized that I was English. 'I'm not saying they got close to the mark; they overstepped the mark. That's why we lost. Victory was decided on something other than the Olympic spirit,' Delanoë declared to the Paris council a few days afterwards, while simultaneously picking up his ball and refusing to play any more, as children do when they lose a game. The real reason for the defeat was much simpler. London had focused its bid entirely on redevelopment, while Paris was proposing simply to reuse existing facilities. The judges had penalized its lack of audacity.

The image of Paris took another hit later that year when two weeks of urban insurrection across the city's suburbs were broadcast live across the world. The trouble began in the isolated town of Clichy-sous-Bois on the evening of 27 October 2005, when three teenagers trying to escape a police identity check ran through a small wood and hid in an electricity substation. Two were killed almost immediately; the other eventually escaped with severe burns. The local population, convinced that the boys had been deliberately left for dead, took their anger and frustration on to the streets.

The police teams involved were cleared of any wrongdoing, but the important thing was that people thought such policies were not only possible but likely. The country's interior minister, Nicolas Sarkozy, had already told residents of a nearby suburb – and the watching media – that he would clean up lawless housing estates with a Kärcher power hose. The sentiment in such disadvantaged towns, mere kilometres from Paris, was that the government considered them a stain that needed to be washed away.

Ten years later little has been done to improve the lives of those in such communities, and the insurrection is starting to be seen as an act of political insurgency rather than an explosion of wild and uncontrolled rage – possibly even with a kernel of genuine revolution. But if there were to be a new metropolis, its limits would be difficult to establish. Although Paris is today dwarfed by its suburbs, the city boundaries have not changed since 1860, when it swallowed up dozens of neighbouring towns and villages. As the historian Colin Jones has pointed out, 'very few observers at that time would have imagined that a city so evidently in a dynamic phase of expansion would be confined within the same boundaries a century and a half later.' It was that same year that Jules Verne had imagined a future Paris, twice the size of today's city and with a population of five million.

The election of Nicolas Sarkozy as president in 2007 at least helped to put the question of an enlarged Paris back on the table. The new leader of the country had put down his Kärcher and wanted to make peace with the suburbs. Paris, with its surrounding towns, was, he pointed out, 'the most economically powerful region in Europe', but development was stalling. 'Do we want Paris, in the next twenty years, to be playing in the first or second division of world metropolises?' he asked in June 2007. For the president, the only way to keep the city in this elite would be to group everyone together into a new 'Grand Paris'.

In *Notre-Dame de Paris*, Victor Hugo had described how the city had previously expanded in the Middle Ages: 'The mighty city had cracked, in succession, its four enclosures of walls, like a child grown too large for his garments of last year.' Paris was very tightly squeezed into the same clothes it had been wearing since 1860, but in 2009 a selection of possible new Grand Paris outfits was revealed.

The designs were by ten teams of architects who had been asked to imagine the future city 'without restrictions or taboos'. Unveiling these first visions at the Cité de l'Architecture et du Patrimoine museum on 29 April, Sarkozy appealed to French pride: 'The real, the beautiful, the great – it's exactly what we want to do with the Grand Paris.' It was a reference, once again, to Hugo, who had used those three adjectives to compare Paris to Athens, Rome and Jerusalem. Naturally, both men placed the French capital above all three.

One of the projects, led by the architect Antoine Grumbach, chose to follow a suggestion made by Napoléon Bonaparte in 1802: 'Paris-Rouen-Le Havre, a single and unique city with the Seine as its main street.' In the mid-twentieth century the French absurdist Ferdinand Lop had also proposed extending the city's boulevard Saint-Michel all the way to the sea, but now the suggestion was completely serious. 'All the Universal Exhibitions held in Paris were organized alongside the Seine, for many reasons,' Grumbach pointed out. 'The Seine is the vector of identity of the metropolis.'

Other projects included gigantic pointed skyscrapers in unlikely corners of the suburbs, futuristic aerial Métro lines above the city's radial motorway, channels of forest marching into the city, and forests of solar panels marching outwards. The artists' impressions looked like science-fiction serigraphs, and seemed as close to becoming reality as Jules Verne's future city.

Before these visions were revealed, Mayor Delanoë had won a second term in 2008 with an increased majority (57.7 per cent of the vote), but he remained reluctant to push Paris towards expansion – and risk once again giving the city the reputation of being the vampire of France. Instead, he pushed on with his previous policies. Soon grey Vélib' bicycles and electric Autolib' cars became a feature of the city, and whole chunks of the riverside expressway were permanently closed to traffic. Delanoë was accused of using his mandate to put in place 'spectacular actions in the service of his own personal glory', but this was partly because he had little other room for manoeuvre – despite having a budget and a staff larger than those of many national ministries.

More than unemployment, insalubrity or insecurity, the biggest problem in Paris was the shortage of housing. During the first ten years of Delanoë's regime, property prices in Paris increased by more than 140 per cent, but the city could not

Vélib' bicycle on boulevard de Sébastopol.

The newly restored glass roof of the Grand Palais.

take the heat off the market. There was simply nowhere left to build. 'What's at stake is finding space, above all for housing . . . we cannot prohibit ourselves from looking upwards,' declared Delanoë, flirting with plans to tear up the city's restrictions on buildings over 37 m (121 ft) high. Thirty years after the construction of the last tall buildings in the city, a ring of skyscrapers around the city edges might help to keep the lowest wage-earners, students and young families in Paris.

Although Delanoë attempted to reassure the population by declaring that skyscrapers would be built only if they respected strict environmental guidelines, he also recognized something else: most Parisians did not want them. New projects were proposed – a large triangular tower at the southern edge of the city, Lego block law courts to the northwest, the redevelopment of the abandoned Samaritaine department store – but each became bogged down in endless debate and digger-stopping legal judgments.

Instead, the *ville-musée* has had to be satisfied with a kind of permanent polishing-up. The Grand Palais was reopened in 2007 after twelve years of painstaking work on its spectacular glass roof; the first floor of the Eiffel Tower had a makeover,

View down the steps
of Montmartre, by Lamarck
Caulaincourt Métro.

which included the installation of vertiginous glass floor panels; and even the scruffy, proletarian place de la République was embellished. Other Parisian squares – Bastille, Nation, Panthéon, Madeleine – also have scheduled appointments with the cosmetic surgeon.

Instead of growing upwards (which might still be a possibility in coming years), the city was confirmed in its outward spread on 1 January 2016, when the Métropole du Grand Paris became a legal reality. Paris's boundaries may still be the same, but it has now grouped its urban, social, economic, environmental, cultural and housing policies with 124 surrounding towns, covering about seven million people. For Paris, this simply recognizes the evolution of the territory over recent decades. In 1989 the journalist François Maspero had already noted the new Paris, a city that had seen the departure of 'craftsmen, workers and small shopkeepers – all the people who went to make up a Paris street', chased away by the higher rents of a glossed-up capital. 'Where had the life gone? To the suburbs. "All around" could not, therefore, be a wasteland, but a land full of people and life. Real people and real life.'

As had been seen in 2005, however, real people and real life also meant real problems in many areas, the forgotten towns created to house those who could no longer afford to live in Paris itself (but many of whom still worked in the city). In 2015 Paris discovered that it too had serious problems. On 7 January two gunmen attacked the offices of the satirical newspaper *Charlie Hebdo* and killed twelve people in and near the building. The terrorists were two brothers, Chérif and Saïd Kouachi, who had been born, brought up and radicalized in Paris.

Eleven months later, on 13 November, the city was once again the target of a horrendous attack, this time on restaurants, cafés, bars and a concert venue, leaving 130 people dead. The attacks in January, targeting cartoonists, were a clear strike against one of the founding concepts of the French republic: *liberté*. The November killings had another target, the *fraternité* of Paris. By carefully choosing venues in the multicultural and festive east of Paris, the terrorists – mostly French and Belgian – targeted a certain way of living in Paris: socializing with people of all origins on the terrace of a bar, listening to rock music or going to a football match.

Although Paris will take time to recover, little by little life has returned to something approaching normality, and Parisians are determined that their city's *joie de vivre* should not be dimmed. Dusted down and tagged on walls, the city's motto began to make sense once again: *Fluctuat Nec Mergitur* – she is tossed by waves, but does not sink.

Parisians have also found some confidence in the way they know best, by imagining new large-scale events. The city is working on a bid to host the Universal Exhibition in 2025, and has entered the race for the 2024 Olympic Games, exactly one hundred years after the city last organized the event. If Paris is successful this time, much of the structure, from the stadiums to the Olympic village, will be built outside the current city limits.

Much of this new infrastructure will be in the disadvantaged but dynamic north of Paris. At the beginning of the twentieth century, the writer Daniel Halévy stood at the top of the Montmartre hill, where he had grown up, and looked out, not towards Paris but to 'this other view, the reverse, which, to the north, spreads out across another city, apparently just as big, an immense city . . . uniform, without steeples or palaces, without history, an unknown city and everything to discover.'

On rue Cortot, rue du Mont Cenis and rue de la Bonne, this view today – despite the grounded flying saucer of the Stade de France, despite the revolving neon advertisement on the Pleyel tower, despite the marching ants on the A1 motorway – could still be described the same way. A staircase leads down from there towards this unexplored city. This way lies the future.

Marianne in mourning: the place de la République in front of the memorial marking the terrorist attacks on 13 November 2015.

THE PLACE DE LA RÉPUBLIQUE

On the evening of 7 January 2015, they came in their tens of thousands. Walking silently, they carried flowers, candles, sketches, pens and pencils. Four days later they could be counted in their hundreds of thousands, filling not just the square but all the surrounding streets and avenues. At the centre was a symbol, a 10-m- (33-ft-) high bronze statue of Marianne, the personification of the French Republic.

The place de la République is not the oldest, the most attractive or the most touristic square in the city, but it has recently taken on a significance that goes beyond the borders of Paris and of France. In part this is because of the terrorist attacks of 2015, which were seen as a strike at the country's constitution, and which took place within hundreds of metres of the square.

Starting life as the location of a large fountain at the end of the eighteenth century, the square did not find its true identity until a century later, when the brothers Charles and Léopold Morice won a competition to build the statue. Nevertheless, the renamed place de la République (place du Château-d'Eau until 1879) always remained slightly askew of the ancient centre of Paris, its cold immensity seemingly more useful as a transport interchange (five Métro lines run beneath it) than as a site of leisure.

It was not until it was given a facelift in 2013 that this image began to change. Although the square had been a gathering point for almost weekly demonstrations throughout the twentieth century, it was always simply a departure point. The new layout, which rerouted traffic and placed the monumental statue of Marianne at the heart of a vast concrete agora, made it a place where people could congregate and stay put.

The attacks of 2015 transformed the statue into something resembling a shrine, a repository for flowers, flags and messages. More recently, the square became a makeshift camp for the Nuit debout movement, a youth protest against employment insecurity. These were not the uses imagined by the architect of the transformation, Pierre Alain Trévelo, but neither are they a surprise. Trévelo chose to leave as much open space as possible, believing that 'emptiness calls for human activity.' For the architect and academic Géraldine Texier-Rideau, 'Répu' is now 'a place where anything is possible, belonging at once to everyone and no-one.'

Although it is difficult today to plot the centre of a city coiled into twenty different arrondissements, its heart is now undoubtedly the place de la République.

A quiet moment on the rue du Nil, 2nd arrondissement.

THE CITY TODAY

Lights Out on the Avenue du Cinéma?

Slightly drowsy in plush leather seats that are said to be the most comfortable in any cinema in Paris, I'm jolted out of my torpor by the sight of a tall, thin man bounding on to the raised area at the front of the auditorium. With a smile almost as wide as the screen behind him, he begins to introduce the film we are about to watch. Although it tipped me out of my slumber, the man's appearance is not a surprise. This is Jean-Jacques Schpoliansky, a familiar figure to all cinema-lovers in Paris. He has run this cinema, Le Balzac, since 1973, but his legendary humour, passion and bonhomie are as fresh as ever. He can almost always be found at his cinema, and he always introduces the films.

Le Balzac, just off the avenue des Champs-Élysées, is one of the last independent cinemas on the city's Right Bank. Since the district is now dominated by international brands, this independence is becoming more and more difficult to preserve, but Schpoliansky is determined to continue his struggle. After the film, he invites me into his small box above the ticket desk. The office also functions as the cinema's archives, and although it is strewn with the clutter of a hoarder, the historic documents and press cuttings are filed carefully into binders. The cinema was opened in 1935 by Schpoliansky's grandfather, and he shows me the articles that were published in the French press the following day. He is clearly proud of this family story, but also keenly aware of his role as preserver of an heirloom. At some point it will be time to pass the responsibility on to the next generation, but it seems unlikely that much will change.

Jean-Jacques Schpoliansky and piles of movie cans.

Inside the projection room at Le Balzac.

Schpoliansky admits readily that computers and social media are not his thing, and although he has staff who look after these, the cinema itself has made little concession to changes in technology. You will not find films shown in 3D here, and he is a reluctant user of digital film.

Schpoliansky looks back with nostalgia on the 1950s and '60s, when Le Balzac pulled in more than 400,000 spectators a year, but he knows that such figures are impossible for anyone today. 'If we have 170,000 spectators in a year – and that over three screens – I break open the champagne,' he tells me, but the story is the same for the neighbouring establishments. The Champs-Élysées boasted 65 screens in 1970, but only 35 remain today. However, Schpoliansky recognizes that France – and Paris in particular – still has an exceptional breadth and quantity of cinemas in comparison to almost any other country in the world.

Of the 911 million tickets sold in cinemas across Europe in 2014, some 209 million were in France. The figure is four times higher than that of the United Kingdom, and 66 per cent of the French population – about 39 million people – went to a cinema at least once during the year. Naturally, therefore, France has the most cinemas – over 2,000 – and the number of seats and screens also rose by over 5 per cent in 2014. Perhaps tellingly, though, the total number of cinemas decreased. The French are still cinema addicts, but they enjoy the experience more and more in multiplexes outside city centres.

Despite losing nearly half its film-showing capacity, the Champs-Élysées still brands itself as the 'Avenue du Cinéma', but the links are becoming ever more tenuous. There is an annual film festival, regular premières are held for films seeking a red-carpet publicity boost, and the post-César Award festivities are hosted by the slightly timeworn restaurant Fouquet's, but there is little in the way of creation, inspiration and negotiation.

For much of the twentieth century, the Champs-Élysées was undisputedly the centre of the French film industry. The connection to the world of the movies was not so much the cinemas themselves – although the street would later be home to the highest concentration of establishments in the city – but rather the film business in its entirety. The cafés of the Champs-Élysées helped it to become the French Hollywood. The growth in the French cinema industry was

Le Balzac cinema on the street of the same name.

The big screen at Le Balzac, venue for numerous special events.

mirrored by the increasing number of bars and restaurants on the avenue, such as Le Select, and Le Triomphe with its steel fountain, water show and live orchestra. In addition to the projects and deals being discussed over a *café crème* or cocktails, all the major producers, distributors and advertising agencies had offices on the avenue. One of the best known to cinema audiences in France was the Jean Mineur agency, with its little axe-tossing animated character and famous Champs-Élysées address and telephone number. So linked did that number become to Mineur that it was put on his tombstone in Cannes: *Jean Mineur, Eden zero, zero, zero, un.*

If the street attracted starlets and silver-screen dreamers, it also drew millions of people who were simply looking for a pleasant evening out. Although today Schpoliansky carefully chooses challenging, mostly low-budget films to show at Le Balzac, cinema-going on the Champs-Élysées was not generally expected to be an intellectual experience. One of the many establishments that are now closed, Le Triomphe (once owned by Schpoliansky's father), projected the soft-core shocker film *Emmanuelle* for 553 consecutive weeks from its release in 1974 to 1985.

The decline came in the 1980s. One by one the smaller independent cinemas closed or were absorbed into the multi-screen chain establishments that are still active on the avenue today. There was L'Ermitage, where a singer called Bétove would perform on stage after screenings, and the Gaumont-Champs-Élysées, its single room decorated in marble, brass and leather, with seats boasting hydraulic suspension. The last screening there was on 31 December 1999, before the cinema was – somewhat typically – replaced by a flagship Benetton outlet.

Given its preponderance in the film industry, it is perhaps a surprise that the street should have been used so sparingly as a location (Jean-Luc Godard's *À Bout de souffle*, or *Breathless*, 1960, is an honourable exception). Perhaps the street's innate, eternal drama played against it, making it a backdrop that would too easily become a scene-stealer. Since the unexplained murder of Philippe Lebon, the inventor of gas lighting, on the avenue in 1804, the Champs-Élysées has always been cinematographic and melodramatic.

It is this power of the visual and the myriad myth-making images that have helped to build the street's prestige internationally: Victor Hugo's body lying in state under the Arc de Triomphe before his pauper's hearse was pulled slowly down the avenue towards the Panthéon; the tear-stained post-First World War parade of crippled survivors; Charles de Gaulle's triumphant city-liberating stride down the avenue in August 1944 (commemorated by the sculptor Jean Cardot at the intersection with place Clemenceau); the annual demonstrations of military might on 14 July, Bastille Day, and even the yellow jersey crossing the finishing line at the end of the annual Tour de France.

It did not begin this way. The 'Elysian fields', originally hunting grounds, were made into a bridle path towards Versailles by Louis XIV in 1667. A promenade leading to the Tuileries in the eighteenth century brought more animation, but it remained sedate. It was in the nineteenth century that

Souvenirs in the Galerie des Arcades.

the Champs-Élysées' reputation was forged, first in the lower part of the avenue, between the place de la Concorde and the Rond-Point (where the Grand and Petit Palais stand today). It was a place of dancing establishments and cafés, which came vibrantly alive in the summer. The polka was invented at the Bal Mabille, which was frequented by Balzac and Baudelaire, but this new avenue also brought crime and prostitution. The bucolic tree-lined thoroughfare prompted the construction of many mansion houses, only one of which stands today. This was the most luxurious of all, the Maison Païva, which was built for an infamous enchantress. Its architect, Pierre Manguin, spent ten years living on-site and overseeing the work, fussily inspecting the installation of the neo-Renaissance onyx staircase and the vermilion bath taps.

Most of the houses have gone, but luxury still survives. The spectacular Louis Vuitton store brings queues of wealthy tourists, and Guerlain – on the avenue since 1912 – sells its Champs-Élysées perfume from an attractive Art Nouveau boutique (perhaps making the Champs-Élysées the only street in the world to have its own scent). Such prestigious links have made the Champs-Élysées the Paris address of choice for multinational companies, transforming it into a street of flagship stores and plush offices. The result is that although 100 million people spend time on the avenue each year, only 82 people call it home.

A tendency to rigid conformity and over-familiar international logos means that the street's drama has been turned down several notches in recent years. Alongside luxury boutiques now stand fast-food chains and shopping arcades, decorated in airport-hub plastic, where the wandering tourist can find tat, titillation and – bizarrely – a deluge of security and spy equipment.

The result, admits Jean-Jacques Schpoliansky, is a street that 'has been abandoned by Parisians'. Le Balzac would probably find life much easier in a different district of Paris, but its owner remains deeply committed to an area that he believes can become a culturally important part of the city again. On a personal level, it is also a place with very strong family links: 'I remember walking here with my father, and it would take us about three hours just to cross the road. He knew everybody.'

Since tourists very rarely visit the cinemas of the Champs-Élysées, the only possible solution is to attract the city's residents back to the street. Le Balzac has had to move beyond just showing films. 'I have a wonderful team who create events, and it is our goal to offer exceptional things every day,' explains Schpoliansky. These events include retransmissions of opera performances from around the world, with champagne served in the foyer, and occasional gastronomic events organized by the cinema's Michelin-starred neighbours.

Elitist, perhaps? Undoubtedly, although Le Balzac still privileges a cinema of passion and protest rather than Parisian intellectual navel-gazing. With the cinema industry having dumbed down a great deal over recent years, Parisians should be thankful for an independent cinema that assumes its audience has a brain – and above all, that it can exist in an area that has slowly lost its soul.

City of Immigration

Walking up to the Palais de la Porte Dorée on the eastern edge of Paris, it is impossible not to be impressed. First, an elegant and exotic avenue of palm trees and fountains leads towards a somewhat incongruous golden statue of Athena. Beyond sits the palace itself, a massive rectangular block, its long, extravagantly sculpted facade partly hidden behind two dozen narrow concrete columns. It's a spectacular building – but one that for most of the second half of the twentieth century was spectacularly embarrassing. Today it houses the Musée de l'Histoire de l'Immigration, but it started life as the focal point of the Colonial Exhibition of 1931, a mammoth event organized to celebrate the wonder and success of the French Empire – just when it was beginning to fall apart.

Reporting on the opening of the event on 7 May, the conservative newspaper *Le Figaro* was breathless in its admiration: 'The visit of the President and Maréchal was graced by moments – in these unique surroundings which showed everywhere the marks of craftsmen, sculptors and pioneers – with the aspect of an apotheosis.' On that opening day thousands of Parisians lined the streets leading to the fair, but not everybody shared the enthusiasm of *Le Figaro*. 'While blood is flowing in Annam, the Vincennes fair was opened yesterday with an imperialist speech by Paul Raynaud [Minister of the Colonies],' headlined the left-wing paper *L'Humanité*. Both newspapers followed the French president Gaston Doumergue around on his inaugural visit. The journalist from *Le Figaro* remarked on the 'dazzling smiles' of the indigenous people, and the 'athletic black musicians'. At *L'Humanité*, the focus was on the 'workers' who would be sweating through twelve-hour days. 'We don't even have toilets,' they pointed out, 'and nowhere to eat either. We eat standing up.'

Throughout the exhibition, the French government aimed to highlight the benefits of the empire to its own sometimes sceptical population. Building the fair in the east of Paris not only involved the embellishment of a run-down zone, but also offered the chance to spread its message to the doorsteps of a population seen as being 'communist' and anti-colonial. As in its colonies, the government felt that its duty was to impose its values on uncivilized natives.

Although morally dubious today, it was certainly a spectacular show in 1930s Paris, a city otherwise in the grip of depression. To see everything, it was estimated that one would need to walk 15 km (more than 9 miles). For those unwilling to cover such distances on foot, there was a train and rickshaws or, for the more adventurous, rides on animals, including elephants, camels and zebras.

The show was open until midnight each day, and visitors were encouraged to come at dusk, when the 3,000 projectors and 1,500 lamps illuminating the installations were switched on. Most impressive of all, particularly at night, was a 50-m-(164-ft-) high, 5,000-sq.-m (53,800-sq.-ft) reproduction of an Angkor temple, representing French Indochina. It was a decor worthy of Hollywood, but even the most dazzling film sets need actors and extras to bring them to life.

Those actors and extras consisted of 1,500 indigenous people from across the empire, recruited not – as had been the case for similar events in the past – as human zoo exhibits, but rather as semi-permanent sales staff peddling typical local refreshments and rustic artefacts. Nevertheless, their movements were firmly controlled, and they had to seek permission to leave the site.

The broadly successful colonial fair came to an end on 24 November, and observers noticed presciently that it also marked the conclusion of something larger. 'The end of the dream', headlined *Vu* magazine, noting the cloud of melancholy that had descended on the site. There would never be another colonial exhibition in Paris. The vast monuments were dismantled and the actors paid and sent back home. The zoo, originally a temporary annex to the fair, was made permanent and moved to the site it retains today. Reclassifying the palace, though, proved more of a problem.

Built as the Palais des Colonies, it slowly took on various other identities (the Museum of France Overseas, the National Museum of African and Oceanic Arts), attracting fewer and fewer visitors, its monumental triumphalism becoming less and less relevant. It was eventually saved by two things: despite the changing face of the museum, the basement has always been home to an ever-popular aquarium; and, when all is said and done, it is a fantastic building (and, since 1987, a listed one).

Ingeniously, at the beginning of the twenty-first century the palace was given a 180-degree twist. Instead of celebrating France's dominance over its colonies, it became the Cité Nationale de l'Histoire de l'Immigration – a place that aimed to 'make the contributions of immigration to France known and recognized'. The palace's collection of art and objects was transferred to the recently built Musée du quai Branly, and a new collection centred mainly on memory and modern creations was curated.

Since the building still visually celebrated the colonies and colonialism, the switch was not a simple one to make. If, as the museum's creators pointed out, 'the history of immigration could not be tied simply to colonialism', there were clear links. However, even at the time of the fair it was apparent that immigration was changing the face of France – and Paris – to a far greater extent than colonialism.

Between 1921 and 1936 one-fifth of the population growth of Paris was down to immigration. In 1921 only 3 per cent of Paris residents were counted as foreigners, but by the early 1930s it had risen to 10 per cent, 'a level no other major European city could match'. This early influx was mainly made up of other Europeans. The hotel kitchen described by George Orwell in his *Down and Out in Paris and London*, written in 1929, is staffed only by Italians, Russians, Hungarians and a solitary Englishman.

The first foreign immigrants had come to Paris in the nineteenth century – bankers from Switzerland, Germany, Brussels and Vienna, such as the Rothschild family – and gravitated mostly towards the top end of society. The real immigration into the city, though, was young men from the poorer regions of France. They gathered in communities, keeping the language, food, habits and clothing of their places of birth.

For many of these young men, it was an immigration representing 'a sort of temporary pact', with Paris developing a reputation as a place of passage. Writing a year after the colonial exhibition, Daniel Halévy noted that provincials still saw the capital as a place without a specific cultural identity: 'Your city . . . is for everyone; you live there for ten years and you become a Parisian; it's a crossroads, a passage, an amusement for the universe; a country is something else entirely.' If Paris were not a country with its own folklore, it was at least a land of welcome.

When the European empires collapsed after the Second World War, France became not a country of immigrants, but

The facade of the Musée de l'Histoire de l'Immigration and Diadji Diop's sculpture . . . *Dans le bonheur*, 2009, resin.

The spectacular interiors of the Musée de l'Histoire de l'Immigration.

certainly a country of immigration. Post-war industrialization coupled with a low birth rate meant that the country needed vast quantities of (cheap) workers, and the newly independent countries could provide those in large numbers. Many people settled around Paris, manning car factories and building sites.

I have come to the museum to find out a little more about these migrations, and to explore the grandiose architecture and implausible interior of the building. I have brought my two children, although they are more attracted by the promise of a visit to the aquarium, and an hour or so in the park opposite – the site of the fair in 1931, but now a playground of rowing boats and pony rides.

They are, however, impressed by the exterior of the palace, and particularly the 1,130 sq. m (12,200 sq. ft) of bas-reliefs carved into the facade by the sculptor Alfred Auguste Janniot. Depicting what the colonies brought to France, and stretching from the Americas to Australasia, to unsuspecting children's eyes it looks much like a three-dimensional storyboard. Among the abundant flora and fauna we pick out crocodiles and coffee, sugar cane and gigantic elephants, as well as the boats and trains that brought everything to France.

Inside, the children quickly run into the Salle des Fêtes, a wondrous room bathed in soft light from invisible windows 27 m (nearly 90 ft) above. Here you can really appreciate the designs of the architect, Albert Laprade, who aimed to represent the empire in condensed form, wrapping an angular Art Deco shell around elements from Moroccan palaces and Asian pagodas. The extravagant frescoes by Pierre-Henri Ducos de la Haille, painted here from floor to ceiling, are a counterpoint to the exterior, depicting instead what it was believed France took to the colonies. These walls, which cover themes including peace, justice, liberty and medicine, along with their cowering and grateful natives, are awkward to experience today, but were already embarrassing when the paint was still fresh. On the fresco representing the Americas, Ducos de la Haille painted a giant skyscraper, provoking Laprade to cry, 'But we don't own the USA!' The painting stayed, however, and remains today.

Climbing to the mezzanine floor above we reach the gallery of donations, an emotion-stirring mix of clothes, passports, sewing machines, musical instruments, photographs and documents, the cherished objects brought on difficult journeys from Poland, Italy, Armenia, Algeria, Mali, Senegal. Visitors are invited to donate their own objects and help to build an ever-evolving collection of tiny stories.

One level above again is the permanent collection, a sequential visit through two hundred years of immigration into France. Sounds follow us around the collection: snippets of conversation in dozens of languages, music, interviews, sporting commentaries and post-match celebrations – the sounds with which we are already familiar in many parts of Paris today.

The collection reminds us that Paris has also traditionally been a land of welcome for the oppressed and for those seeking greater freedom of expression or in their choice of lifestyle. Much of French culture is built on such openness: the work of Chopin, Picasso, Chagal, the École de Paris, photographers such as Brassaï and Kertész, Josephine Baker, even Uderzo (Italian) and Goscinny (Polish), the creators of the authentic French icon Asterix.

'Are you an immigrant?' my children ask me. They are both born-and-bred Parisians, and occasionally tease me for my accent and grammatical errors. There was of course no mention of the English in the building. There has never been an English diaspora, even though Paris – and France as a whole – has thousands of English inhabitants. My move to France was not one of desperation and necessity, but simply a lifestyle choice. It would be difficult to explain to them how I became primarily a citizen of Europe and Paris, rather than British, but my privileged situation is far simpler than that of dozens of the parents of their school friends. Paris is a city of immigration, but not one of the world's great melting pots, mostly owing to a French republican insistence on preserving a shared secular identity. France demands greater assimilation than other societies, but integration is not easy when you live cut away from society in ghettos. 'I suppose I am,' I reply, 'but a very lucky one.'

After visiting the aquarium and eating an ice cream, we hire a boat on the lake opposite. At the colonial fair, this lake took visitors from Madagascar to Laos, but the islands then packed with attractions are now peopled with sunbathers. All around us, laughing, relaxing, playing, kissing, is the face of a multicultural city, a sight worthy of a palatial celebration. Beyond the barrier of the fair, though, in the thickets of the Vincennes woods, new immigrants from the ruins of colonialism are sleeping in tents under the trees. There is still much building to be done in Paris.

The New Belly of Paris

In March 2014 the local media – and members of the Paris food scene – gathered on the rue du Vertbois, near the place de la République, to celebrate an extravagant new initiative. Behind it all was one man, Cédric Naudon, a mysterious young French businessman who was said to have made a fortune in property in the United States. A complete unknown before the launch, he made a remarkable entrance in a designer suit, silk scarf and chauffeur-driven Maserati.

His project, La Jeune Rue (a name taken from a poem by Guillaume Apollinaire), involved the transformation of 36 empty shop units in the rue du Vertbois and the neighbouring rue Volta and rue Notre-Dame de Nazareth, all of them apparently purchased by Naudon himself. Reclaiming the area from the dominant wholesale textile units, there would be a fishmonger, a grocer, a cheese shop, a butcher, a cake shop, bistros, a market, galleries – even a cinema. All would be supplied by the best natural and sustainable producers across France, without the intervention of any intermediaries. Finally, each unit would also be remodelled by one of the world's leading interior designers.

The French magazine *L'Express* declared it to be the 'nouveau "Ventre de Paris"' (the new 'Belly of Paris'), but a year later the project amounted to a single restaurant that was sunk by debts and a shortage of clients. Flicking through Émile Zola's novel of that name, I find a passage that could help to explain the failure of the project: 'Since the beginning of the century only one original building has been erected, only one that is not a copy from somewhere else but has sprung naturally out of the soil of our times, and that is Les Halles,' Zola wrote of the original Paris belly. The Jeune Rue project may have insisted on ethically sourced local produce, but in the rue du Vertbois, nothing had grown organically.

La Jeune Rue came as an invader, a parasite, to a street that was anything but young. Another developer had tried to breach the neighbourhood in the nineteenth century, proposing to demolish the tower and fountain after which the rue du Vertbois is named (and which can still be seen where the street meets the rue Saint-Martin). City protector Victor Hugo gave his typically droll judgment: 'Demolish the tower, no . . . demolish the architect, yes.'

Today the street is already home to a slightly offbeat community, including a luthier, a fashion designer, a yoga centre and several establishments serving the local Jewish community. Above all, it shelters one of Paris's food monuments, L'Ami Louis, at number 32, a place that could never have entered into Naudon's scheme. Instead of La Jeune Rue, here is a restaurant that is the very image of *le vieux Paris*.

L'Ami Louis chose to ignore the noisy new neighbour and carry on as normal, although Naudon spotted the blocking point – or opportunity – during the launch of the project. 'We'll get it in the end,' he declared to journalists, hungrily eyeing what would have been his *pièce de résistance*. Perhaps unsurprisingly, the old hand outlasted the young upstart.

The restaurant may not even have noticed what was going on outside. It seems, after all, hardly to have noticed the passage of time since the nineteenth century, living happily as a museum piece frequented mostly by American tourists. Very few Parisians would be prepared to pay €70 for a *poulet-frites* (chicken and chips), especially one served up by gruff men surrounded by a decor akin to 'a second-class railway carriage in the Balkans'. L'Ami Louis is the complete antithesis of a modern approach to food and dining. 'It is, all things considered, *entre nous*,' wrote A. A. Gill in *Vanity Fair*, 'the worst restaurant in the world.'

And yet it is regularly full, an old piece of comfortable furniture that typifies Paris and its cuisine in the eyes of many visitors. Jacques Chirac entertained Bill Clinton there in 1999, the two acknowledged *bon vivants* tucking into plates of foie gras, snails and cold duck slices. Establishments such as L'Ami

Louis, though, with their chequered tablecloths, white-jacketed waiters and moth-eaten menus, are helping the Paris food scene to slide rapidly down influential world rankings.

'Paris has come to be regarded as a dull, predictable food city,' wrote Michael Steinberger in the *New York Times* in 2014. Alongside the trusty but staid classic institutions, a recent report in France noted that as many as 70 per cent of the restaurants in the country were serving ready-made frozen meals produced off-site in large industrial kitchens. 'The real surprise was that anyone was surprised,' Steinberger added, before going on to point out that France is McDonald's' second most profitable market in the world.

The Parisian brasseries and bistros dishing up reheated *plats du jour* are also places that breathe history, whose walls have absorbed decades of cigarette smoke and the vapour of stimulating conversations. The white tablecloths, the familiar friends on the menu, the slightly greasy cutlery, the idea that generations of writers and artists have sat in these same seats before you: it's an integral part of the Paris myth, and one that will not be easily shaken up.

It is a similar story at the Paris markets. Sometimes housed in magnificent iron halls, sometimes running deliciously down the centre of a boulevard, their colourful piles of produce are a wonderful and tempting sight. Most of these goods, though, have come from the real new *Ventre de Paris*. When the centuries-old Les Halles market in the centre of the city was shut down in the 1960s, a new food metropolis was built out in Rungis, near Orly airport. Market traders queue each morning – alongside supermarket negotiators – at the same centralized suppliers.

It wasn't always this way. For hundreds of years, producers came by horse and cart to Les Halles each morning to sell their own produce. The towns surrounding Paris had their own specialities – peas in Clamart, peaches in Montreuil, asparagus in Argenteuil – and different streets around the market were known for different foods. Medieval Parisian market-goers were consumers of an early street food, tasting perfectly carved goose served with a rich broth at the porte Saint-Merri, or pork sausages on the rue de la Saunerie. Everywhere there was an odour of puréed peas, hot broad beans and garlic sauces.

Such scenes and aromas helped Paris to develop an international reputation for its gastronomy. In 1570 the Venetian visitor Girolamo Lippomano noted, 'The French spend on nothing else as willingly as on eating, and to make what they call *bonne chère*. This is why the butchers, meat traders, roasted meat-sellers, resellers, cake-makers, cabarets and taverns are found in such confusing quantity.'

In 1769 an almanac listed 590 'traiteurs, aubergistes et hotels garnis' where it was possible to eat. These were forerunners of the restaurant, an invention that was truly a 'phénomène Parisien'. Many were grouped around the Palais-Royal, notably the Café de Foy, 'the biggest, the handsomest and one of the most honest', from where the French Revolution would shortly spring.

The city's reputation continued to grow in the nineteenth century. An early guidebook, the *Almanach de l'etranger à Paris* (Almanac for the Foreign Visitor to Paris) of 1860, summarized the breadth of the culinary offering: 'Of all the cities in the world, Paris is the one where people eat the most in restaurants; it is the city where we can eat the best fare if we do not consider what we spend; it is also the capital where we can best eat at very moderate prices.'

By the 1920s and 1930s, though, as the food historian Patrick Rambourg points out, 'French cuisine had settled into a comfortable lethargy where innovation was banished.' Possibly connected, this period coincided with the arrival of the influential *Michelin Guide*. For the last hundred years, this rather dry red book and its powerful system of stars has always privileged sumptuous settings and conservative food. In 2010 this mummification of French cuisine was further cemented when 'the gastronomic meal of the French' was officially recognized by UNESCO as part of the world's cultural heritage – making it by definition untouchable.

In recent years, though, chefs have begun to fight back against the power and influence of the *Michelin Guide* and its ratings. Although acquiring a Michelin star is undoubtedly still the best way to attract customers to a restaurant, it also means employing more staff and lowering the inclination to take risks.

One of those who rebelled was Alain Senderens, who renamed his three-star restaurant on the edge of Paris's Golden Triangle and announced that he was making it more affordable and more casual. In doing so, he gave up his hard-earned stars. 'I cannot continue to pay two waiters to carry a dish and a third to take off the lid,' he proclaimed.

Celebrating this new simplicity and spontaneity is a movement called Le Fooding, with an associated magazine of the same name, which, apart from mangling the English language (blending together 'food' and 'feeling' to create a word that is difficult to swallow), has helped to promote a new concept of eating in Paris. According to the essayist Adam Gopnik, 'Le Fooding was to cooking what the New Wave was to French cinema.' In essence, he continued, 'eating with a new attitude was as important to Le Fooding as actually eating something new.'

Walk a few streets west of the rue Vertbois, past the prostitutes of rue Saint-Denis and the fashion wholesalers of the Sentier, towards what remains of Les Halles, and you arrive at the rue du Nil. Without any fuss or noise, without any extravagant claims or flashy designs, it has perhaps succeeded in doing what Naudon set out to do, and become a recognized culinary centre of the capital.

Much of this is down to one chef, Gregory Marchand, who trained under Jamie Oliver in London and went on to work in New York before settling in Paris. Marchand claims that this experience knocked the traditional French basics out of his system, enabling him to focus instead on fresh produce and the integration of new flavours. The success of his first restaurant – Frenchie, for the nickname he was given by Jamie Oliver – has enabled him to open a wine bar and the even more casual Frenchie To Go. Others sharing his philosophy have been attracted to the small street, including Terroirs d'Avenir, a shop specializing in high-quality produce direct from the farm.

The rue du Nil now possesses an authenticity that has disappeared from the neighbouring district of Montorgeuil, a channel running off the original Les Halles market. Chefs wander up and down between each of Marchand's establishments, and can be seen working on the day's recipes, the tempting odours wafting out of the open windows. One can almost imagine the broad beans and garlic sauces of the Middle Ages.

New dining in Paris: Frenchie on the rue du Nil.

Le Fooding has championed many other young chefs: the Basque Iñaki Aizpitarte, the American Daniel Rose, Adeline Grattard, who blends Asian influences into her cuisine, and Bertrand Grébaut. All of them have set up restaurants in simple old café-bistros outside standard Michelin territory, often combining limited-choice taster menus with natural wines from small, independent producers.

'Like the New Wave filmmakers,' says Gopnik, this new breed of chef 'had a vague sense of what they wanted, combined with a vigorous determination to achieve it, whatever the hell it was.' Food in Paris did not have to mean a toss-up between starched extravagance and a lazy leaning on familiar classics; a dose of un-Parisian modesty and simplicity coupled with passion and generosity could cook up something new. This perhaps explains why La Jeune Rue was spoiled before it ever reached the table.

Le Dimanche Parisien

On market days, the escalator leading out of the place Monge Métro station delivers you right into the middle of the stalls. As I ascend slowly on a radiant Sunday morning, the market is already tickling my senses. Rectangular awnings and clusters of thick green leaves frame a square of blue sky, and just before I reach the surface, a bouquet of odours hits my nostrils. Breathing in, I already know that somewhere I'll find cut flowers, banks of fish, pungent cheeses and bunches of fresh herbs.

A note above all these, though, is the aroma of roasting chicken. Just from the rich tang I can clearly picture the birds lined up on skewers, dripping their fat on to piles of shiny peeled potatoes in the tray below. It's an archetypal Parisian Sunday scent, and the place Monge market is a thoroughly Parisian Sunday experience.

'I want there to be no peasant in my realm so poor that he will not have a chicken in his pot every Sunday,' Henri IV is said to have proclaimed during a discussion with the Duke of Savoie at the beginning of the seventeenth century. The famous remark is probably apocryphal, but the Sunday chicken remains a Parisian staple nevertheless.

Around the place Monge – a few streets away from the Latin Quarter – the majority of the population can afford even the most thoroughbred of hens, even though this was not so long ago one of Paris's least prosperous areas. When he arrived in Paris in 1921, Ernest Hemingway lived at nearby rue Cardinal Lemoine, an address that, he declared, 'could not have been a poorer one'.

George Orwell, who was down and out nearby in rue du Pot de Fer, would concur. His hotel was 'a dark, rickety warren of five storeys, cut up by wooden partitions into forty rooms', where 'long lines of bugs marched all day like columns of soldiers, and at night came down ravenously hungry, so that one had to get up every few hours and kill them in hecatombs.'

Hemingway wrote of a time when mandarins froze overnight in his draughty, unheated top-floor apartment, and when goatherds announced the arrival of their troupe in the street below by blowing their pipes lustily, calling local residents down for fresh goat's milk that was squeezed directly into their pots.

The area has maintained its connection with food, but it is many years since a herd of goats has been seen there. The scene is a lot less pastoral today, and the market a more typically urban experience, even if place Monge is far from being the boisterous souk seen across Paris in Belleville or Barbès. The stallholders here do not shout to attract customers, but instead chat to the families who return each Sunday. Those families come not for the prices – with a few rare exceptions, markets in Paris are not places to pick up bargains – but for the quality of the produce. There are the earthy cheeses, bunches of carrots still carrying the mud they grew in, boxes of satisfyingly misshapen tomatoes, unpolished apples and pears, long stalks of pink-flecked rhubarb, and piles of unfashionable turnips. For a touch of the exotic, there is even bubbling chicken *mafé* on the market's African food stand.

The place Monge market, which began in 1921, is far from being the city's oldest or largest, but, positioned around a pretty fountain, it is quite possibly the quaintest. It could easily be the focal point of a small – wealthy – provincial town, if it were not for the fact that it is also overlooked by the gloomy but respectfully solid Garde Républicaine barracks.

Follow the walls of this building to the rear entrance and you arrive on the ancient rue Mouffetard, part of the original Roman route to Lyon and Italy, and 'hearty and sprawling like a sow'. The shops on this street are all open on Sunday morning, a historic exception to city laws that allow the *commerces de bouche* (food traders) to operate until 1 pm. For Hemingway, rue Mouffetard was 'that wonderful narrow crowded market

Sunday shopping at the Marché Monge.

street', and although chain stores and other trappings of
gentrification have muscled their way in, it is still a lively
Sunday morning experience.

The road leads gently down to the church of Saint-Medard,
giving the neighbourhood a further air of provincial spruceness.
The traditional Left Bank bourgeois families can still be spotted
there, gathered on Sunday for mass and then a procession of
baptisms. Their pristinely coiffed offspring in floral dresses or
shirts and tailored shorts are playing in the square, the epitome
of the very particular French verb *s'endimancher* – to dress up
in your Sunday best.

On the other side of the square, the accordionist Christian
Bassoul is running through his repertoire of French *guinguette*
classics. For the last forty years he has led *le p'tit bal de la rue
Mouffetard* each Sunday morning, a singing and dancing
session in the shadow of the church. The audience contains
a few curious families, their young children delighted with
the unexpected permission to dance in the street, but most
of the hardcore participants are a couple of generations older.

As the bakers, butchers and greengrocers begin shutting up shop and packing away their unsold goods, the bystanders return home for a hefty lunch, possibly with members of the extended family. Together they might later take a stroll to the nearby Jardin des Plantes, one of the oldest and most Parisian of gardens, where perhaps they will visit one of the museums and eat ice cream. Afterwards they will return home to finish their schoolwork or prepare the evening soup. This, at least, seems to be the vision of Anne Hidalgo, the mayor of Paris.

Hidalgo's declared aim is to defend what she calls the *art de vivre parisien*. 'I've always been against the generalization of Sunday opening, because such generalization would mean the death of small shops,' she declared at a press briefing in November 2014. Instead, she launched a social-media campaign informing Parisians what they could – or perhaps should – do on a Sunday, ranging from going to the cinema to helping their children with their homework.

It was a curiously anachronistic campaign, a painting of a city based on the holy Sunday trinity: rest, food, family. For anybody not in the place Monge demographic, it is easy to share the sentiment of the writer Jean-Paul Clébert, who

Sunday shopping at the Marché Monge.

declared, 'I hate Sundays' when writing about the Mouffetard district in the 1950s.

For three hundred years, Sunday has meant many different things to Parisians. When the Council of Trent declared the Sabbath to be sacred, in the late sixteenth century, the Parlement de Paris went even further. Swearing and blaspheming were declared to be illegal on Sundays, with a fine for the first offence, six hours in the stocks for a second, and a piercing of lips or tongue for a third offence. Sundays, unsurprisingly, became unpopular, and so connected with the Church and the aristocracy that during the French Revolution the day was abolished, to be replaced by a *decadi* every ten days. Revolutionary laws stated that workers could organize their time as they liked and choose the day of rest that suited them best. However, instead of 52 Sundays a year, people now found themselves with only 36 *decadis* and five public holidays. Since citizens were encouraged to spend their *decadi* in civic instruction and learning about their obligations, this quickly became another controlled and dull day to dread. The Gregorian calendar – with its more traditional Sunday – was reinstated by Napoléon Bonaparte in 1805.

Reborn, Sundays became synonymous with feasting and celebration. Whole families went to the *guinguettes* or cabarets shrewdly situated just outside the city walls (where they paid fewer taxes). These rustic and verdant venues not only offered cheap food and drink but also satisfied, as Guy de Maupassant wrote, 'this thirst for a rural ideal that haunts Parisians in spring'. Paintings such as Georges Seurat's *A Sunday Afternoon on the Island of La Grande Jatte* (1884) and Renoir's *Luncheon of the Boating Party* (1881) captured typical scenes.

The family Sunday – rather than the religious Sunday – was a bourgeois invention, but it was not until 13 July 1906 that it was legally designated an official day of rest for everyone in France. Saturdays did not follow as a generalized day off until the 1970s (when a worldwide economic depression forced a shorter working week), which explains why the French still use an Anglicism for a previously unimagined concept: *le week-end*.

On Sunday afternoon at the place Monge the last traces of the market have been washed away by street cleaners. A Guignol puppet show has attracted a few families to the square, but there is little animation elsewhere. Rue Mouffetard is far livelier, its antique charms attracting tourists in search of Hemingway or just somewhere to shop, drink or eat.

This, too, is typical of a Paris Sunday. Across the city many places are open, but just as many are closed, without it being entirely clear why that should be the case. According to French law, work allowed on a Sunday covers everything 'necessary', anything related to culture (cinemas, theatres and museums) and – more ambiguously – work that is considered to be 'reasonably pleasant'. Shops should in theory be closed, but exceptions are made in areas deemed to be important for tourism, although this idea has now stretched beyond the Marais, the Champs-Élysées and Montmartre to some depressingly mundane shopping centres as well as the principal department stores.

Since Paris is an important international city and a prime weekend destination, this would seem to make economic sense, but the fear of many in the city is that it will lead to the 'banalization' of Sunday. A century or so ago, however, 'it was this commercial animation that distinguished so agreeably the French Sunday from the greyness and boredom of an English Sunday.'

Back at the now empty and silent place Monge in the evening chill, the eternal problem with Sunday is heavy in the air: that it is followed by Monday and the start of a new working week. As the twentieth-century photographer Robert Doisneau – who would have appreciated the banality of the weekly market scene – wrote, 'on Sunday morning we've got all day, but already in the afternoon the presence of the factory starts to form in the mind.'

It's about time I took the Métro back home and got started on the soup.

Le Meurice hotel.

A Palace in Paris

In 2010 France's secretary of state for tourism announced the creation of the Palace, a new luxury label for the country's hotels. The classification, specific to France and valid for a period of five years from the award of the label, guarantees a level of luxury greater than five stars, with particular attention to the hotel's position, architecture, history and interiors as well as the size of the bedrooms and the quality of the food and drink on offer.

Although Americans still represent the largest single group of visitors to France, this classification targeted a newer clientele. The ministry is well aware that future growth will be found among the nouveau riche in China, India and other Asian countries. Better still, statistics suggest that these individuals tend to come with fatter wallets that they open slightly more readily than the more longer established visitors.

Of the sixteen hotels in France that have been awarded this distinction, eight are in Paris. Several more establishments – including such prestigious names as the Ritz, the Crillon and the Lutetia – are currently undergoing renovations with the aim of obtaining the label. In essence, the Palace classification moves the city's luxury accommodation one step higher, with an un-avowed aim of competing with new international destinations. Indeed, with an offshoot of the Louvre in Abu Dhabi, branches of Chanel and Louis Vuitton shops in Dubai, and an Alain Ducasse restaurant in Doha, Paris has even begun to compete with itself, but in locations geographically closer to the new demographic, where hotels are often larger and more luxurious.

At Le Meurice, the oldest of all the Paris Palaces, such concerns hardly seem to register. The hotel was quick to apply for the Palace classification, but it was seen as a necessary minor adjustment rather than a revolution that, in any case, would probably be counterproductive in such an establishment that trades on its conservatism. The best way for the hotel to adapt, its management seemed to conclude, was simply to remain as it has always been. Describing itself as 'the Parisian pied à terre of the privileged', and situated directly opposite the Tuileries gardens, near the city's principal designer boutiques, Le Meurice was already ideally positioned to capture such a clientele. The hotel also prides itself on the services it offers, which go as far as providing toy boats in hotel colours to sail in the ornamental pond in the Tuileries, and devising a special menu for babies that allows them to choose whether they would like their meat and vegetables steamed, grilled or sautéed.

Keeping children happy is one thing, but, as with other luxury establishments, the real goal is attracting the ultra-wealthy and encouraging them to be loyal. One of the principal arms in this battle is the hotel concierge, an individual – still primarily a man of a certain age – who will become a long-term friend, adviser and confidant. 'There are some guests who book their visits around my availability, checking first that I will not be on holiday when they want to come,' Jean Mora, deputy head concierge at Le Meurice, tells me as we discuss the hotel and its guests in its plush gold-plated Dalí restaurant. 'Some people come here for several weeks at a time, and it is like a second home to them. They know all the staff by their first names, and we get to know them and their needs very closely too.'

It is teatime when we meet, and a waiter brings over some madeleines still steaming from the oven. Infused with honey and thyme, they are probably the best I have ever tasted, and it is easy to see how – with a few million in the bank – one might quickly become accustomed to such surroundings.

Mora is clearly proud of the connections he has managed to create over time with the hotel guests: 'We have one couple who will shortly be celebrating their 100th visit here, and another guest who has stayed with us 800 times!' Calculating average room prices in my head, I quickly estimate that this must amount to an investment of over €1 million in the hotel, but I imagine one simply doesn't mention money in an establishment such as this.

Meeting Jean Mora provides me with my first opportunity to enter Le Meurice. The Parisian Palace hotel is not my normal environment, but Mora instantly makes me feel at ease. The hotel seems smaller than I had imagined, but also more welcoming. Since its opening, in 1835, this 'home from home' approach has been an integral part of its modus operandi. Augustin Meurice, who founded the original establishment in Calais, and then its spin-off by the coach terminus in Paris, specifically tailored it to meet the needs of the English, providing the bathrooms and English-speaking staff that were traditionally difficult to find in France. Today the British still come, but Americans have long made up the bulk of the guests.

It is easy to see how Mora establishes long-term relationships with people from a culture built on the provision of service and frank communication, but I wonder how he is adapting to the new clientele from cultures with more formal and coded rules. 'For us it is a challenge and an objective to get to know each new client, wherever they are from,' he explains. 'We have someone on our staff who speaks Mandarin and can provide a service to our Chinese guests. There are of course cultural problems with the establishment of these relationships, and it is not always simple. The Russians at first had their whole itineraries planned by agencies, and never used the concierge, but now they are slowly starting to come to us. The Chinese use agencies as well, but I think within two or three years they will come to us too. In any case, it is our job to adapt to every client at the hotel, whatever their needs may be.'

'Paris is still all about fashion, gastronomy, shopping – and the beauty of the city,' Mora points out when I ask if new visitors require new diversions. 'Most people still come for these things, even if for certain people – the Chinese, for example – shopping and luxury brands are much more important than food.'

The Palace, therefore, is an integral part of the Paris brand – offering luxurious French interiors, top-class restaurants and views across the city itself – but there is also a certain irony in the fact that little of this now belongs to France. Le Meurice is today part of the Dorchester Collection, owned by the Brunei Investment Agency. It is the same story for the competition. The Shangri-La is part of a chain of hotels based in Hong Kong, and the Peninsula is also Chinese-run. As Mora points out, though, when considering a hotel such as Le Meurice you should really look at the bigger picture. Owners come and go, but the hotel itself – specifically its history – is almost untouchable. 'We celebrated our 180th anniversary in 2015. This is not to say that the hotel is old-fashioned, but it is not "fashionable" either. It is more of a timeless place. The life story of this mansion is still very visible,' he declares, giving me a tour of some of the Louis XV-influenced interiors, and pointing out elements of decoration – sofas with swans' necks for arms, tables with shoes on their feet – influenced by its long-term resident Salvador Dalí, who regularly spent one month a year in the hotel.

Mora tells me some of the legends: how Dalí would give staff small change to throw in front of his car when he left the hotel, simply so that he could *rouler sur l'or* (drive on gold); and how he paid page boys in cash for each fly they managed to catch in the Tuileries gardens. At other times he was more creative. He once invited the press to his suite, and then proceeded to throw bags of paint from the balcony on to the street below. This was his 'explosion' painting, and also one of the first 'happenings' to be organized in Paris.

Given these famous precedents, I ask if today's clients are still as imaginative – and particular – in their demands. 'Yes, of course,' Mora answers, 'but our guests today are far more reasonable than Dalí! We once had to send a member of staff to London to collect a certain brand of cat food, and once bought a special brand of sketching pencils for a Middle Eastern prince – a regular client – who had sent his Boeing from Spain to collect them. We also had a guest from Saudi Arabia who replaced all the French-style furnishings in his room with furniture he had sent over from Saudi Arabia, but we have long experience of such requests in this hotel. King Alfonso XIII of Spain also brought his furniture with him when he stayed here in exile in the 1930s.'

A concierge is a confidant, someone to whom customers often confess things ('like a barman', Mora points out), and this entails a certain vow of secrecy. Mora therefore cannot tell me any of the outlandish or illegal requests he has received, but he does reveal that customers sometimes ask for firework displays to be organized across Paris, or to land their helicopters in the Tuileries. 'This is of course impossible,' he confirms.

If anything is changing in the presentation of the Paris brand to the top end of the tourist market, people such as Mora will be the first to feel the effect. Yet, although visitor demographics are evolving, he doesn't believe that his job will change very much in the near future. 'The job of a concierge will always be based on personal relationships,' he says. 'I cannot imagine there ever being a cyber concierge!'

Already, though, new technology is making the world smaller, and the hotel's guests are far more savvy about Paris than they used to be. The concierge, who previously acted as guide and organizer for clients lost in the city, now rarely plans complete itineraries. However Paris – and the world of tourism – changes, one thing will remain constant: the importance of the concierge's address book. 'Of course', Mora assures me, 'it is still easier to get reservations in certain places using the concierge than if you tried by yourself.' I now have his card safe in my wallet.

Paris by Night

It's 11 on a Friday evening and I have a rendezvous on the Île de la Cité. The temperature rose to nearly 35°C during the day – enough to warp train lines in the outskirts of the city – but since the sky cracked in thunder and sent down buckets of water, the mercury has dropped quickly. In two weeks' time it will be the longest day of the year, and the sky retains a few streaks of daylight. But then Paris – city of light pollution – never gets very dark.

My rendezvous is with Sylvanie de Lutèce, Paris explorer and part-time DJ, who will be leading a small group of us on a nocturnal tour of the underbelly of Notre-Dame and the Île de la Cité. The walk promises tales of murder, prostitution, alchemy and devil-worshipping. Suitably, the meeting point is next to the city's main police station.

The event has been organized as part of a Paris City Council-sponsored programme called Les Nuits de Paris, which aims to prove that the city still has a vibrant and varied nocturnal culture. Curiously, it shares its name with the first book about the city's nightlife, written by the self-proclaimed *hibou-spectateur* (spectator-owl) Rétif de la Bretonne at the end of the eighteenth century. The programme's organizer, Sandra Berkoukeche, assures me that this was not intentional, and – since the 'night owl' spent 1,001 nights in the city observing bodysnatchers, wife-swappers, murderers, rapists, cross-dressers, executioners, gamblers and suicides – it is understandable that the authorities did not want to draw any allusions.

Nevertheless, I can't help feeling that Rétif de la Bretonne would have enjoyed following Lutèce's tour. The night – 'the best moment to seize the soul of the city' – is not the subject of our adventure, but it does provide the ideal stage set. 'The night is made for poets, lovers, patrols, thieves and novelists,' wrote Alexandre Dumas in *Les Mohicans de Paris* (The Mohicans of Paris) in 1854, and most of these characters seem to be gathered in front of Notre-Dame on this Friday evening, alongside tourists taking selfies, whom Dumas somehow overlooked.

'You have to imagine it teeming with life here,' declares Lutèce, struggling to make herself heard over the sounds of scratchy guitars, djembe drums, tinny stereos and cackling groups of teenagers. With her tricorn hat, she looks the part, but making the psychological jump back a few hundred years is not easy. In the Middle Ages we would have been guided towards Notre-Dame by the *porte-falot* or lantern-carrier, but today we are snaking across the parvis holding illuminated balloons.

In the days of Rétif de la Bretonne, the Île de la Cité was 'more an inextricable maze than a town', and one of the most miserable parts of Paris. Our guide points out the traces of this 'barbaric and gothic Cité' that remain etched into the parvis: miniature ancient churches, rotting taverns and houses built practically on top of one another. Beneath our feet, the crypt contains even older remains – the foundations and chunks of old Roman walls, when the Île de la Cité was 6 m (20 ft) lower than today's island. Rétif de la Bretonne would not recognize it today. 'We choke here,' he wrote in the 1790s. 'The air doesn't circulate; it feels like walking at the bottom of a well.' Tonight on the excessively large parvis created by Georges-Eugène Haussmann in the 1860s, the air is circulating a little too easily and we have to pull up coat collars and tighten scarves.

As we shuffle up to Notre-Dame itself, Lutèce gives us an esoteric reading of the facade. Most visitors do not attempt to decipher the hidden hieroglyphics on the church's skin, despite generally having ample time in seemingly endless queues. She points out the devils, the suicidal monks, the alchemist – even Lilith, the biblical Adam's first wife. Although

Sylvanie de Lutèce's night-time tour of the Île de la Cité.

this is the city's most important Catholic church, its facade hides dozens of enigmatic and distinctly unreligious messages carved by anonymous medieval sculptors.

At midnight the illuminated facade is suddenly plunged into darkness. The church is clearly no night owl, but even that seems somehow significant. During an event that is supposed to highlight the city's nocturnal culture, Notre-Dame has already tucked herself up comfortably for the night and blown out the candle.

The tour carries on under street lamps to a police garage on the site of a fourteenth-century building. Alongside the cars and motorbikes, a trace of ancient foundations can be found in the basement. We are told that it could be the only remaining sign of a barber's shop and neighbouring patisserie where unsuspecting students had their throats slit before being transformed into pâté.

Finally, Lutèce – who knows all the entry codes and buttons to press – takes us down a dark, narrow alley to the location of an old church crypt. Only two pillars remain,

Outside Notre-Dame on Sylvanie de Lutèce's night-time tour of the Île de la Cité.

now absorbed into later buildings, but most surprising of all are the tombstones that have been transformed into paving stones. Smoothed by centuries of footsteps, the names of people who must once have been important local figures are still just about readable (by the light of a mobile-phone screen).

'Always be curious. Open doors and look around you. You never know what you might discover,' Lutèce encourages us. This might be a description of Paris's night-time experience, but, as if on cue, a man pops out of his ground-floor apartment and reminds us that it's half-past midnight and that he'd like to sleep. It is fine to be curious at night in Paris, as long as you are also silent and invisible.

Paris is winding down and the Métro will shortly stop running, but not everyone is ready for bed. Crossing the Seine back to the Right Bank and home, I stop and look upstream. In the cramped, gnarled medieval city, the wide and open river offered the only good view of the sky, and tonight it doesn't disappoint. In medieval Paris, nobody would have been outside at this time. 'At night the gates were shut, the river was barred at the two extremities of the town with massive iron chains, and Paris slept tranquilly,' wrote Victor Hugo in *Notre-Dame de Paris*. For the deeply religious inhabitants of Paris, night was a glimpse of hell, a land populated by dangerous animals and highwaymen. As something to experience, night in Paris only really began in the eighteenth century.

By the nineteenth century, the writer and adventurer Alfred Delvau declared midnight in Paris to be 'a delicious hour during the summer, when the night owls are only just beginning to breathe and live.' In comparison, in provincial villages it was still the time when the ghosts come out. Such night-time excesses may not be good for the health, but there were many, like Delvau, who believed that it was 'better to die at thirty in Paris than at one hundred in a village'.

Day and night began to offer alternative ways of living in Paris. Even the words in French began to seem significant (*le jour*, solid and masculine, and *la nuit*, feminine) – like Paris herself, at once enchanting and entrancing. The night was an antidote to a rather conservative society, enabling Parisians to relax and feel a little less restrained. In daylight hours, the city was the capital of work and speed. By night, 'when men cease to be machines', it became the capital of hedonism.

In 1842 a popular song declared 'Voilà Paris la nuit, du plaisir et du bruit', and the city's boisterous ribaldry began to establish Paris as the world's nocturnal capital. Sensing this danger, leaders of the Second Empire and Third Republic looked into ways of abolishing the night altogether. Darkness encouraged immoral behaviour, but in an industrial age sleep was also seen as a waste of time. In 1889 a proposal for the city's Universal Exhibition (won in the end by the Eiffel Tower) was to build a giant 360-m- (1,180-ft-) tall lighthouse. The declared goal of this *colonne-soleil* was to project eternal daylight over Paris.

If we wind forward 150 years, it seems that sleep has won the day – or rather night. Paris's reputation for nocturnal exuberance was cemented in the nineteenth and twentieth centuries in the cafés on the Grands Boulevards, the cabarets of Montmartre and the bars of Montparnasse. Until the 1980s nightclubs such as Le Palace and Les Bains Douches were attracting jet-setting partygoers, but recent night-time trends have not been so spirited.

In 2009 a group of exasperated musicians, bar owners and DJs launched a petition under the label 'Quand la nuit meurt en silence' (When the night dies in silence). For them, Paris had its finger to its lips, and local rules were 'relegating the city to the rank of European capital of sleep'. It was to counter this image that events such as Les Nuits de Paris were created. Outlining the main goals, Berkoukeche told me that it aimed 'to show that the night in Paris isn't only about clubbing but also about concerts, theatre, walks, museums and sport'. Perhaps more tellingly, she also pointed out the importance of the city's nocturnal reputation to its overall attractiveness. 'Paris nightlife helps the city's prestige to grow internationally,' she admitted, but, in common with many things in the city, it represents a delicate balancing act.

The city authorities seem to have a wildly varying attitude to the night, encouraging venues to play the game on officially sanctioned dates, but then to turn down the volume during the rest of the year. It is for this reason that one of the city's liveliest streets, the rue Jean-Pierre Timbaud in the 11th arrondissement, just to the south of popular Belleville and Menilmontant, also chose recently to make a gesture.

On 21 June each year France celebrates the Fête de la Musique. It is the only time when music can be played almost anywhere, all night long, and for the city's bars it represents the opportunity to rig up an amp and order extra stocks of alcohol. In 2014, however – even though the event fell on a profitable Saturday night – most bars on rue Jean-Pierre Timbaud elected to keep their shutters firmly rolled down as the rest of Paris partied.

I end my evening on this very street, a few blocks from where I live. It was near here that I first encountered Lutèce, recounting boisterous tales of night-time gangsters and fallen women, events that used to take place on dark nights in the neighbourhood. It is far calmer today, although small groups of young men and women are gathered outside the bars, laughing and talking at volumes that counterbalance the music ringing in their ears.

Is Paris still a night-time city? The question might have seemed trivial, merely to do with lifestyle, but it became far more important after the attacks of 13 November 2015. The terrorists killed blindly, but they also sought to silence the nocturnal city. Since then Parisians have begun to see nightlife as part of the city's DNA, and as such something to defend, but fear is still keeping many at home. In the nineteenth century Delvau wondered 'what noise will the world make the day that Paris shuts up?' We can only hope that we never find out.

Passages through Time

To the Surrealist writer Louis Aragon, the Paris *passages* – glass-covered arcades dedicated to shopping, entertainment and refreshment – were 'sanctuaries of a cult to the ephemeral'. The fleeting name itself was already a magnet to Aragon, 'as if, in these corridors undressed by the light, people were not allowed to stop for more than an instant'. Aragon, along with his fellow Surrealist André Breton, spent much time in the passage de l'Opéra, one of several that would be torn down in the post-Haussmannian redevelopment of the city at the beginning of the twentieth century. The two men delighted in the 'ghostly landscape of pleasures and cursed professions, unintelligible yesterday and which tomorrow will never know', taking care to record all the idiosyncrasies and just plain ordinariness they observed.

These 'human aquariums' fascinated the Surrealists because they were convinced that such environments would soon be erased from the city completely. Their flame had burned brightly but, it seemed, for only a very short time. At first as modern, light and airy as railway terminals and exhibition halls – 'all constructions with transitory aims', as Walter Benjamin pointed out – they rapidly came to be seen as poky and dusty alongside the new luxurious and well-stocked *grands magasins* department stores, where the shopping classes spent entire leisurely afternoons.

Even in the 1920s – about a hundred years after they first appeared – the arcades had seemed to Aragon 'already dead in their primitive life', and had continued simply as a kind of living museum – a fact that rendered them all the more enchanting in a world dedicated to modernity. Their existence, though, was vital in the development of the philosophy of Breton and Aragon. 'The father of surrealism was Dada,' declared Benjamin; 'its mother was a gallery called passage.' Nearly a hundred years later again, a returning Aragon would be flabbergasted to discover that not only have the passages survived, but in many cases they are thriving, even if they still present a slightly skewed-in-time vision of Paris.

Mostly centred on the Grands Boulevards – the pleasure parade of nineteenth-century Paris – the principal *passages* trace a line down the centre of the city, leading towards the Palais Royal and the prototype wooden passage, the Galeries de Bois. Each passage, the result not of careful planning but of rampant speculation, has retained or developed its own identity, making for a fascinating walk that has the advantage of being pleasant in all weather.

From the north, this line begins on the medieval curve of the rue du Faubourg Montmartre, a stone's throw from the Haussmannian hubbub of rue La Fayette. The gated entrance to the passage Verdeau stands like a portal to this antique world, rather appropriately, since this particular passage has become closely linked to the nearby Drouot auction house. passage Verdeau, which opened in 1846, remains an impressive construction of glass and iron, despite decades of dust and a labyrinth of cracked floor tiles. A central artery in the Quartier Drouot, it is home to several antique shops and antiquarian booksellers, their premises crammed floor to ceiling with rare editions and obscure, forgotten volumes.

Immediately across the rue de la Grange-Batelière is the passage Jouffroy, which possesses a different look and atmosphere from the passage Verdeau, despite having the same promoters and architects. It is slightly cleaner and better kept than its smaller neighbour, probably because it is also home to the perennially popular Musée Grévin waxworks gallery. Since the museum's exit is in the passage itself, the regular procession of families has encouraged a specialization in vintage toy shops, cafés and sweetshops.

Passage Jouffroy.

The passage echoes like an indoor swimming pool to the shouts of sugar-filled children, and the warm light that gently falls from the glass ceiling also seems to encourage thoughts of a quick dip. There is no water here, but there are other services. Two clocks, for example, demonstrating once again that the Paris passage is a place for people in a hurry. More remarkable still, there is also a place to sleep – the Hotel Chopin. Room 409, which offers a plunging view of the glass canopy roof, is said to be a particular treat for fans of covered passageways.

Encircling the exit of the Musée Grevin are shops selling theatrical kitsch and tourist tat, but there is one treasure in the passage Jouffroy: the showroom for Fayet, a producer of walking sticks based in the suburbs of Paris and a supplier to pedestrians across the world, from Japanese emperors to Dr House. At the beginning of 2015, the company took over the unit from the Segas brothers, traders in walking sticks who had been operating in the passage for forty years. The walking stick was for generations the ideal accessory for the passage *flâneur*, and now, although somewhat outmoded – like the passages themselves – it still apparently has its fans. 'It is a typically French phenomenon,' explained Gilbert Segas. 'We have walking sticks and the English have umbrellas.'

The showroom, crowned outside by a huge moose's skull and dressed in suitably gothic hues of green and purple, has an exceptional range. In the window is a python-skin walking stick priced at €8,700, but inside more affordable models contain built-in swords or mini bottles and glasses. In the nineteenth century the artist Henri de Toulouse-Lautrec kept a stock of absinthe in a similar model. There is also a walking stick with the head of Charles de Gaulle, and the range of skulls and skeletons seems particularly appropriate.

On the opposite side of the grumbling boulevard Montmartre is the passage des Panoramas, perhaps the archetypal Paris passage and certainly one of the most successful. The Panoramas were giant circular painted frescoes, up to 50 m (164 ft) in diameter and 16 m (53 ft) high, displayed inside two rotundas. Spectators paid 1f50 to stroll down the dark tunnels

Librairie Paul Vulin at the passage Jouffroy.

– the ancestors of the passage – leading to the rotundas, and then placed themselves in the centre of the circular scene, which was lit from above. The most impressive painting showed a view of Paris from the Tuileries Palace, and the effect was reportedly spectacular: 'the result is a certain confusion . . . the more we think about it, the more we are persuaded that we are in the presence of reality,' wrote one witness. Built and promoted by an American inventor, Robert Fulton, they were demolished in 1831.

Despite the gaudy Victoria Station pizza restaurant at the entrance, its eccentric interior based on vintage train carriages with sprung seats and metallic luggage racks, the passage des Panaromas has become a destination for food-lovers. There is heavy lunchtime footfall here from the neighbouring banking sector, but in addition to the fast food and *prix fixe* restaurants there are several that also attract the evening and weekend crowd. Passage 53 meticulously blends Japanese and French cuisine; Racines – 'roots' – offers simple bistro dishes and natural wines, and Noglu, as the name suggests, is 100 per cent gluten free.

The most flagrant example of the change of purpose and direction of the passage des Panoramas is the Caffè Stern. For more than 150 years this shop housed an engraver, but in 2014 it was transformed into a chic Italian restaurant. The interiors are by the ubiquitous designer Philippe Starck, but since the shop is a protected historic monument he had little room for manoeuvre. A winged wolf wearing a necklace in the window is the most visible alteration.

Stern the engraver may have gone, but several shops dedicated to collectors – once the passage's main trade – still survive. Alongside specialists in postcards, autographs, coins and even champagne capsules, there are the inevitable stamp traders. 'O philately, philately: you are a most strange goddess, a slightly foolish fairy,' noted Aragon of these typically superannuated passage dwellers.

The rear exit of the passage was lopped off in the 1920s and incorporated into a luminous development by the hygienist-architect Henri Sauvage. Perhaps that is why the basement also contains a gay sauna, which promotes itself as 'le sauna le plus Rome-Antique de Paris'. Perhaps there is stiff competition among classically themed establishments in the city.

To continue along the seam of the passages one must now skip along rue des Panoramas, down rue Feydeau (the name of another old and now demolished passage) and then south along rue Vivienne, past the Neoclassical Palais Brongniart (the city's old stock exchange), to the Galerie Vivienne. At the entrance is a passage standard, the second-hand bookshop. In baskets outside sit an eclectic mix of titles at €2 apiece, a study on mental illness alongside a biography of Bill Gates, a text on oriental carpets back-to-back with a tutorial on a forgotten computer language. 'In case of absence, slide the money for the books under the door,' announces a card in the window. The world of the passages is truly unique.

This also begs a question. Does the Paris passage attract a certain type of shopkeeper, or does the passage eventually transform each one into a certain type of shopkeeper? The photographer Robert Doisneau noted their exceptional nature, pointing out that in the passages 'there are people who seem a little different too, different to those who live in the dazzling light.' The writer Jules Romains described something similar: 'The passage shelters them and envelopes them in a softness that is almost domestic.'

The Galerie Vivienne – too chic to be a simple passage – is probably the city's finest covered walkway, with Neoclassical decor that dignifies and disguises its commercial activity. Although there are vintage bookshops, toyshops and cafés (in this case the thoroughly bourgeois tea shop A Priori Thé), the passage also specializes in art galleries and showrooms for fashion designers. Although sometimes a little draughty on blustery autumn days, it has warm wooden fittings and swirling mosaic floor tiles by the nineteenth-century Italian artist Giandomenico Facchina that bring a reassuring hug. Further snugness and sustenance can be found at Lucien Legrand, filles et fils (daughters and sons), a prestigious wine retailer that was founded in 1880.

Opposite the Galerie Vivienne is the tiny passage des Deux-Pavillons, barely more than a staircase down to the Palais-Royal. This corridor takes the curious explorer back to the beginning of the story, to the birthplace of the Paris passage.

The Palais-Royal became a veritable fun palace in the 1780s when Philippe, Duke of Orléans – a cousin of Louis XVI – added wooden passageways housing cafés and boutiques. These Galeries de Bois became famous across Europe, attracting aristocrats and dandies, shoppers and revolutionaries. The restaurants were the best in Paris and the boutiques sold – indeed dictated – the latest fashions. But as the sun dropped, the atmosphere changed, for better or for worse. 'The poetry of this amazing bazaar shatters at nightfall. It is horrible and cheerful at the same time,' wrote Balzac. The shops and cafés attracted visitors, but it was the brothels and gambling dens that really enthralled them.

The arrival of another member of the Orléans family on the French throne in 1830 put an end to the fun. Louis-Philippe

– despite being the grandson of the creator of the passage – transformed it into an elegant but extremely dull establishment. 'If morality was a winner, the animation was lost,' noted the journalist Nestor Roqueplan with regret. 'It was the world's bazaar, now it is only a moral, cold, straight, constitutional monument.'

Originally designed to profit from a Parisian obsession with shopping and strolling, the passages bring in little money these days, and although they are now protected, they are condemned to struggle on in the shadow of the city's past. 'What is the future of the passages if not to cultivate their own nostalgia?' wondered the passage explorers Jean-Claude Delorme and Anne-Marie Dubois in 1996. Aragon would be delighted to learn that any kind of future is possible at all.

Two Wheels on the Waterfront

The River Seine, lifeblood of Paris, flows gently from east to west through the city for approximately 13 km (8 miles). It splits the city in two, although the Right and Left banks remain stapled together by 37 bridges. This watery landscape, the poet Léon-Paul Fargue wrote, is 'a unique country, long and narrow, a kind of curved ribbon, an imaginary peninsula that seems to have jumped from the imagination of a fantastic creature.'

In a spirit of urban adventure, I have decided to cross this country, from one border to the other, uniquely along the Left Bank and using only the city's free Vélib' bicycles. Where possible I will cling to the quayside, because, as Fargue added, 'nothing is more Parisian than the quays of the Seine, nothing is more in its place, nor in its setting.'

The route I will follow is already enough to spark reverie. 'These names: Orsay, Mégisserie, Voltaire, Malaquais, Gesvres, aux Fleurs, Conti, Grands-Augustins, Horloge, Orfèvres, Béthune and place Mazas are sufficient history and geography for me,' declared Fargue. In addition to these subjects, my voyage will take in industry, engineering, art, science, education and political power. All this against a trio of adversaries: the heat (the thermometer is pointing above 30°C), pollution and the Parisian motorist.

The starting point is the Vélib' station by the tram terminus on the pont du Garigliano, a functional bridge from the 1960s named after a Second World War battle. On one side of the bridge are the Paris suburbs, their most visible landmark the glass chimney of the leading private television company, TF1. On the other side is Paris and the shiny, squat offices of the main France Télévisions public television network. The bridge already seems to mark a certain divide.

From the bridge, the road slides immediately downhill, giving a first rapid glimpse of the Eiffel Tower. A cycle path, its painted bikes and arrows nearly rubbed away by three lanes of incessant traffic, leads towards the quayside. It is a non-space of car parks and pleasure-boat docks, but quiet, except when trains clatter past on the raised railway track that runs along-side. Beside me is the Seine and her 'lovely green dress / And her golden lights.' It suddenly occurs to me that I am cycling against the flow of the river, perhaps even against the energy of the city. 'She is leaving for the sea,' wrote the poet Jacques Prévert, 'Flowing like a dream / In the middle of the mysteries / Of the miseries of Paris.'

The path leads up to the Parc André Citroën, visible under the concrete arc of the railway line. With one of the largest expanses of grass in the city, two huge glasshouses and a tethered balloon, it is difficult to imagine that this area, known originally as Javel, was once home to a chemical factory (the name became synonymous with bleach, a product that is still known as *eau de Javel* today), and then a car factory. After the

Vélib' velo station.

Citroën plant closed in the 1970s, it was slowly transformed into today's rather wonderful park.

A few more revolutions of the wheel, past building depots and cement silos (the Seine in Paris is still very much a working river), bring me to the pont Mirabeau, an ordinary bridge rendered forever poetic by Guillaume Apollinaire. The poet often crossed this flat, green iron bridge when visiting his lover, the painter Marie Laurencin, and in his mind this river span and the ever-flowing Seine came to symbolize their break-up: 'Sous le pont Mirabeau coule la Seine/ Et nos amours / Faut-il qu'il m'en souvienne / La joie venait toujours après la peine.'

It may be water under the bridge, but clearly the quantity would never be sufficient for Apollinaire. There are surely very few people who create romantic associations with the Front de Seine, a controversial riverside development of tower blocks from the 1970s. From the comfortable seat of my bicycle, the buildings manage by some illusion to dwarf the Eiffel Tower. The angular, multicoloured structures have few fans, but they do house some of the most expensive apartments in Paris and a rather snazzy – but generally largely empty – shopping centre called Beaugrenelle. This is also a good spot to check in and check out the Vélib', ensuring that I stay within the free 30-minute limit.

A little further along is a ubiquitous backdrop for fashion and film shoots, the double-level pont de Bir-Hakeim (named after another Second World War battle). When one has scooted past the bridge, the immensity of the Eiffel Tower always comes as something of a shock, perhaps even more so when on two wheels. Trying to concentrate on the road with thousands of tonnes of iron on your shoulder should in theory be simplified by a cycle path, but in front of the tower the route is blocked by the squadrons of *vélo-taxis* and tuk-tuks that seem recently to have taken over Paris.

The tower stands on the Champ de Mars, named – suitably – after the Roman god of war. This was the site of the original Battle of Lutetia, when Roman invaders crushed the local Gauls. For most of its existence afterwards it was a military zone, a place of parades and practice. 'Must we deduce that the first acts accomplished by men in a certain place impregnate it forever?' wondered Maurice Druon. As I pass by, the day after the 14 July festivities, the faint whiff of fireworks still hanging in the air would seem to suggest so.

After the crowds and metallic mass of Eiffel's structure, the Musée du quai Branly, all vertical vegetation and glass walls, comes as something of a bucolic relief. For another kind of relief, the Musée des Égouts de Paris – the sewer museum – is a little further along. The road continues towards Les Invalides and the Assemblée Nationale, but I promised myself that I would stay close to the river. The Left Bank is the city's memory, its schools and its publishers, but at the riverside it was for a long time dedicated to trade, the giant wheat- and coal-carrying barges roped to the imposing walls, the quayside swarming with carts, horses and dockers.

As early as 1901, the historian and diplomat Gabriel Hanotaux was wondering if this picturesque part of the city could not be improved. 'On these banks, could we not, without disturbing the shipping and trade, place lawns, gardens? In these gardens, could we not establish restaurants, dance halls, cafés, convenient benches?' More than a century later, that is exactly what the city authorities have done.

The new Berges de Seine development boasts a floating garden, full of picnicking schoolchildren, several trendy bars and restaurants – some floating, some in the old riverside tunnels – outdoor games and any number of comfortable benches (and Vélib' stations). The installation is on the Left Bank, but the view is across to the Right Bank: the garish pont Alexandre III pointing to the gleam of the Grand Palais, the pont de la Concorde with its blocks salvaged from the Bastille prison, the Egyptian spike of the place de la Concorde, the green of the Tuileries and the outlandish length of the Louvre sliding into the distance.

It was under the bridges on this quay that Léon-Paul Fargue asked the *couche-dehors* (outdoor sleepers) why they favoured this part of Paris. 'Because . . . we're more at ease and at home here,' one man replied. 'What's more, dreams here are more distinguished.'

Bouquinistes along the Seine.

Listening to the river gently slap the quay, a breezy warmth on closed eyes, it is almost possible to imagine yourself dosing on some deserted island. This is no tropical beach, but in the 1930s, when Fargue told his tales of Paris, people did still swim in the Seine. On sultry summer days, he noted, female *bouquinistes* – riverside booksellers – often took a plunge in the river:

> Someone strolls along the quays, for books, and often also to see a dripping mermaid in a bathing costume step out of the water. And he shouts: 'Hey, little lady, how much for the Taine?' In a few strokes, the little lady reaches the bank, picks up her bathrobe, climbs up to the book stand while drying her hands on her hips, sells the Taine, a Flaubert or a Jean Lorrain to the customer, then returns to the cool water.

The weather is scorching today, but I'm not tempted to do the same.

The *bouquinistes* are part of Paris's riverside mythology. Originally the boxes were awarded to injured war veterans or the fathers of large families. Paying only 65 francs a year for their box, they could make a good living. They were allowed to sublet the boxes when they grew old or ill, but could never sell the business. Today the *bouquinistes* sell very few books, instead using their picturesque positions to deal in tourist trinkets, postcards and love locks.

The Berges de Seine come out by the Musée d'Orsay, but immediately there is an unpleasant surprise for those on bikes: on the quai Voltaire, cyclists travelling east are guided over the pont Royal to the Right Bank. It might be possible to push on regardless, but I don't want to suffer the same fate as the absent-minded Pierre Curie, who in 1906 was crushed by a horse and cart a little further along on the quai des Grands Augustins. Since there is no question of crossing the river, I choose to make a detour through the Latin Quarter, away from the Seine but into the historical heart of the city. From time to time I'm rewarded with a glimpse of the river and of Notre-Dame.

The boulevard Saint-Germain angles back down to the river by the Institut du Monde Arabe, a convenient Vélib' swap stop and the perfect place for a break. The architect Jean Nouvel's spectacular glass block had a very difficult gestation period and is still underperforming in terms of visitor numbers, but it is one of the city's lesser-known gems. The ninth-floor terrace offers one of the best (free) views of Paris, from where the flow of the Seine gently draws the eye down to Notre-Dame.

From the terrace you can also see the tourist boats struggling upstream, then happily returning with the flow after they have passed the easternmost tip of the Île Saint-Louis. Paris becomes less classically beautiful beyond this point, but is not without interest. The riverside Musée de Sculpture en Plein Air is uninspiring unless the afternoon or evening dance sessions are taking place, but it is still preferable to the concrete blockade of the Jussieu campus. Further along, the cyclist catches the pungent animal whiff of the Paris menagerie, and then the sweeter scent of the Jardin des Plantes, one of the city's oldest gardens.

Beyond the Gare d'Austerlitz, the Left Bank has developed a kind of post-industrial chic, typified by the Cité de la Mode et du Design, a 1920s warehouse now dressed in a green plastic plug-over. Although it today houses a fashion school and stylishly distressed cafés and bars, it still displays its concrete skeleton proudly. At river level, the clatter of an improvised skate park is noisy alongside the tents of the homeless. On the top floor is another rooftop terrace with impressive views and equally eye-popping prices. In summer months the quay here is a continuous strip of outdoor cafés and terraces, often spilling out from fantastic boats that include a bright red lightship, a Chinese junk and a floating swimming pool. Safely away from residential buildings (a rarity in Paris), the quai François Mauriac has become one of the city's leading late-night spots.

Opposite this land of booze, appropriately, is Bercy, once the kingdom of wine distribution in Paris. Even as late as the middle of the twentieth century, barges were bringing

The Bibliothèque nationale de France.

A floating café-concert by the Seine, with the passerelle Simone de Beauvoir on the left.

thousands of litres into the city from Burgundy, the boatmen almost as full of wine as their barges:

The custom is that each man has at his disposal a barrel of wine for the trip. That might seem excessive, but on the banks where they stop it is the exchange currency for their daily needs; they are given fish, bread and meat, which they pay for with full bottles. Not all of it is loose change though – far from it. A boatman on the Seine easily drinks in a day, without the slightest trouble, five or six litres of wine.

Stretching out to the edge of the city is the new Paris Rive Gauche, the largest urban development in Paris since Haussmann's time. Most visible from the river is the Bibliothèque nationale, its four angled glass towers, representing open books, no longer a surprise in the cityscape. Originally standing quietly alone, the national library is now surrounded by a huge community of converted industrial units and surprising new buildings. This is not an isolated and artificially imposed landscape, but a community that in a few short years has grown healthily around intelligent infrastructure.

One such development is the Jardins Grands Moulins Abbé Pierre, a lively park that segues seamlessly into a university campus, itself artfully housed in a converted flour mill and warehouse. This is where I park the Vélib' for the last time, before continuing on foot to the edge of Paris. Just alongside the tramway – which would take me right back to the beginning, to the pont du Garigliano, around the perimeter of the city – stands the first skyscraper to be built in Paris for forty years. Crooked like an infirm old man, it nevertheless refuses to shock in this environment.

The smoking chimneys and industrial landscape that are visible from the pont National show me that I have come to the edge of my territory, the opposite end of the 'imaginary peninsula'. It was a journey of seven Vélib' pit stops in just under three hours, but now I need a drink. Tomorrow I might attack the Right Bank.

Le Bon Marché escalator.

LISTINGS

SITES

Eiffel Tower
Champ de Mars, 75007, www.toureiffel.paris

Beginning as a ridiculed structure with a limited lifespan, the Eiffel Tower today dominates Paris both as a monument and symbol. Although its height gave it a second life as a radio and communications tower, it remains an empty shell that simply allows visitors to admire the rest of Paris.

Notre-Dame
Parvis Notre-Dame, place Jean-Paul II, 75004, www.notredamedeparis.fr

The cathedral of Notre-Dame, which took more than two hundred years to build, is one of the world's Gothic masterpieces. The centre of spiritual and judicial life in the city for hundreds of years, it was sacked and nearly sacrificed during the Revolution, before being reborn following a campaign led by the writer Victor Hugo.

Montmartre
18th arrondissement

From shrine to artists' village through to today's magnet for tourists, Montmartre has always fascinated and attracted. It was a small town outside Paris until 1860 and has managed to retain a provincial atmosphere, despite widespread development and the more recent arrival of designer boutiques and upmarket hotels.

Versailles
RER Versailles Rive Gauche

The royal hunting lodge transformed by Louis XIV into a vainglorious megastructure and thriving aristocratic community was designed to function as a counterpoint to Paris, and played that role until the end of the nineteenth century. The chateau and gardens are so vast that a whole day is required to get an idea of the place, but even then you won't come close to seeing everything.

Père Lachaise cemetery
16 rue du Repos, 75020

The cemetery was opened in 1804 just outside the city walls, and struggled to attract plot purchases until the city of Paris moved the remains of Molière, La Fontaine and the legendary lovers Héloïse and Pierre Abélard there. The bucolic, restful atmosphere makes it feel like a garden.

Canal Saint-Martin
quai de Valmy, quai de Jemmapes, 75010

The city's second waterway is unrecognizable today from its past as a grimy industrial conduit and the location of one of Inspector Maigret's most gruesome murder investigations. Such associations have been replaced by a swathe of cool and colourful bars, cafés and boutiques. Tranquility can be found in a remarkable 17th-century hidden garden in the neighbouring Hôpital Saint-Louis.

The Marais
between the Hôtel de Ville, the Bastille and place de la République, 75003/75004

Created as a new, upmarket community in the seventeenth century, this part of Paris was later transformed into a semi-industrial zone. Today it incorporates many different identities, including quiet old houses by the river, an effervescent gay community, the ancient Jewish settlement and a more bourgeois family atmosphere in the 3rd arrondissement.

Jardin des Plantes
57 rue Cuvier, 75005, www.jardindesplantes.net

Established as a medicinal herb garden by Louis XIII's physician, the gardens have been open to the public since 1640. Although it still features floral displays and plant nurseries, the park is today better known for being home to numerous museums, as well as the city's menagerie.

La Villette

Métro Porte de Pantin and Porte de la Villette, 75019, www.lavillette.com

When the city's meat industry left Paris in the 1970s, the reclaimed land was transformed into a postmodern park by the architect Bernard Tschumi. It boasts a popular outdoor cinema festival in the summer, concert venues and a large science museum.

The Latin Quarter

Métro Saint-Michel, 75005

The Left Bank is the oldest part of Paris, and is traditionally where the population of the city has learned. The atmosphere is today more kebab and chain store than May 1968, but glimpses of the quarter's past can still be found, notably at the Musée de Cluny and the churches of Saint-Julien le Pauvre (sheltered by the city's oldest tree) and Saint-Séverin.

MUSEUMS

Musée du Louvre

place du Carrousel, 75001, www.louvre.fr

The Louvre was built by Philippe Auguste as a fortress at the beginning of the thirteenth century, and rebuilds, renovations and alterations have been constant throughout its history. It has been estimated that you would need about 150 days to see the 35,000 creations in the museum, but even a bite-sized visit is an inspiring and rewarding experience.

Musée Carnavalet

rue des Francs-Bourgeois, 75004, www.carnavalet.paris.fr

Focusing on the history of Paris, this labyrinthine museum is housed in one of the Marais' most elegant and historic buildings, the home of seventeenth-century letter-writer and wit Madame de Sevigné. The permanent sections are free to visit. Currently closed for renovation until the end of 2019.

Fondation Louis Vuitton
Bois de Boulogne, avenue du Mahatma Gandhi, or via the Jardin d'Acclimatation, 75016, www.fondationlouisvuitton.fr

The Foundation, designed by the American architect Frank Gehry, gives prominence to video installations in its cavernous basements, although its rooftop promenades are as much of an attraction for many visitors.

Palais de Tokyo
avenue du Président Wilson, 75016, www.palaisdetokyo.com

Originally built for the ill-fated Universal Exhibition of 1937, the Palais de Tokyo has vast interiors and extremely high ceilings that give plenty of room for all kinds of installations by the world's leading artists. The state-funded institution shares a café, shop and outdoor space with the city of Paris's **Musée d'Art Moderne**, which has an impressive free permanent collection and is housed in the eastern wing of the building.

Musée d'Orsay
rue de la Légion d'Honneur, 75007, www.musee-orsay.fr

In the 1980s the Gare d'Orsay railway station was transformed into a museum celebrating nineteenth-century art. It is enduringly popular and worth the wait in the snaking queues outside.

Centre Pompidou
place Georges Pompidou, 75004, www.centrepompidou.fr

Richard Rogers and Renzo Piano's once controversial multicoloured, inside-out construction, is today an iconic Paris landmark. Housing the French State's collection of modern and contemporary art (the largest in Europe), it also welcomes successful temporary shows by superstars of the contemporary art world. Furthermore, it offers a spectacular view of the city from the top floor.

Musée des Arts et Métiers
rue Réaumur, 75003, www.arts-et-metiers.net

This museum of science and technology is housed partly in a church that was seized during the Revolution. The transport display in the old chapel, complete with Montgolfier models, early Blériot aircraft and prototype Peugeots, is particularly impressive.

Musée de Cluny
6 place Paul Painlevé, 75005, www.musee-moyenage.fr

Although a rather archaic and confusing experience, this museum gives a fascinating insight into two little-known periods of Parisian history: the Middle Ages and Roman Lutetia. It includes such masterpieces as the tapestry known as *The Lady and the Unicorn*, but it is the huge brick *frigidarium* that is most surprising. A relaxed place to visit, and rarely too busy.

Musée de la Vie Romantique
16 rue Chaptal, 75009, www.vie-romantique.paris.fr

Home of the painter Ary Scheffer in the nineteenth century, this small museum, just off the main Pigalle drag, focuses on temporary shows on a Romantic theme. During the summer months, lunch or afternoon tea in the museum's café – and garden – is a must.

Musée Rodin
79 rue de Varenne, 75007, www.musee-rodin.fr

Reopened in November 2015, this celebration of the work and creative processes of one of the world's best-known sculptors is arguably the city's most impressive museum.

Musée Picasso
5 rue de Thorigny, 75003, www.museepicassoparis.fr/en/

The decision, a year after Picasso's death, to give a home in the Hôtel Salé to works donated to the French State by the artist and his heirs was an inspired one. This beautiful Marais mansion house, refurbished once again between 2011 and 2014, is the perfect location for Picasso's many and varied creations.

HOTELS

Mama Shelter
109 rue de Bagnolet, 75020, www.mamashelter.com/en/paris

Enjoy smart decor at low prices in this Philippe Starck-designed hotel in a converted multi-storey car park alongside an abandoned railway line. The restaurant and rooftop bar are also worth the detour.

Solar Hôtel
22 rue Boulard, 75014, www.solarhotel.fr

Describing itself as 'ecological, economical and militant', this clean and bright hotel to the south of Montparnasse belies its one-star rating. The fixed room price includes an organic breakfast and free use of bicycles.

Hôtel Hospitel
1 place du Parvis Notre-Dame, 75004, www.hotel-hospitel.fr

Functional and basic, but ideally placed on the Île de la Cité alongside Notre-Dame. It also occupies a wing of the Hôtel Dieu hospital.

Maison Souquet
10 rue de Bruxelles, 75009, www.maisonsouquet.com

Proudly proclaiming a past as a Belle Époque 'pleasure house', this boutique hotel plays up to the Pigalle myth with a sensual but tasteful decor. If you prefer, you can simply play chess in the cosy *salon de thé*.

Hôtel de l'Abbaye
10 rue Cassette, 75006, www.hotelabbayeparis.com

Provincial, leafy calm in the heart of Saint-Germain makes this courtyard hotel an ideal spot for those who want to combine relaxation with thriving city life.

ENTERTAINMENT VENUES

Opéra National de Paris

Palais Garnier, place de l'Opéra, 75009; Opéra Bastille, place de la Bastille, 75012, www.operadeparis.fr

Charles Garnier's neo-Baroque opera house is almost a theatrical performance in itself. Affordable tickets can be difficult to find there, but are generally easier to come by at the Opéra Bastille, the city's second (and much more modern) opera house.

Philharmonie de Paris

221 avenue Jean-Jaurès, 75019, www.philharmoniedeparis.fr

A striking recent addition to the Paris skyline, the long-awaited Philharmonic Hall is also revolutionizing classical music in the city by attracting a younger and more diverse audience to concerts.

Accor Hotels Arena

8 boulevard de Bercy, 75012, www.accorhotelsarena.com

The city's biggest multi-purpose arena, a postmodern mix of glass and steel, was recently reborn in a previously unheard-of incarnation in Paris – a venue with naming rights. Major rock concerts are interspersed with events such as tennis tournaments and indoor motocross.

Olympia

28 boulevard des Capucines, 75009, www.olympiahall.com

Long established as Paris's primary music hall, the Olympia has hosted everyone from Édith Piaf to the Beastie Boys.

Parc des Princes

24 rue du Commandant Guilbaud, 75016

Starting life as a velodrome at the end of the nineteenth century, this stadium is today home to the wealthy Paris Saint-Germain football team (although it is still owned by the city of Paris), and an excellent venue to watch a match.

Hippodrome de Longchamp
2 route des Tribunes, in the Bois de Boulogne, 75016, www.france-galop.com/en/node/64

Jam-packed with a chic crowd a couple of days a year (notably for the Prix de l'Arc de Triomphe, each October), this vast and elegant hippodrome is for the rest of the time home to a straggle of hardcore racing fans.

Cirque d'Hiver
110 rue Amelot, 75011, www.cirquedhiver.com

Built in 1852 by the architect Jacques Ignace Hittorff, this spectacular building has hosted circus troupes ever since. The shows – an enduringly and curiously popular form in France – remain largely unchanged in format, and are heavy on performing animals.

Lido
116 avenue des Champs-Élysées, 75008, www.lido.fr

Mixing showgirls, singers, vaudeville and lashings of water in a somewhat kitsch potpourri, a Lido show is a fun if somewhat pricey experience.

Comédie Française
1 place Colette, 75001, www.comedie-francaise.fr

The country's historic State-run theatre employs a permanent troupe of actors to perform classic French plays by Molière, Racine and Corneille, and more recent creations.

Left Bank cinemas
boulevard Saint-Michel, 75005

Almost no other city in the world can boast such a concentration of cinemas as that found around boulevard Saint-Michel on the Left Bank. Certainly none can match the range of classics and avant-garde contemporary films that are typically projected in the district's twelve cinemas.

RESTAURANTS

Frenchie
5–6 rue du Nil, 75002, www.frenchie-restaurant.com

This popular restaurant was named after the nickname the chef Gregory Marchand was given when he worked under Jamie Oliver in London. Expect to find French classics with an international twist. Marchand's empire has expanded to include a fast(er) food café and a wine bar, all in the same small street.

Le Chateaubriand
129 avenue Parmentier, 75011, www.lechateaubriand.net

The Basque chef Iñaki Aizpitarte was one of the originators of the now ubiquitous no-choice taster menus. His impeccable technique and audacious combinations have made this restaurant one of the most difficult to book in Paris, and ensure its regular high placing in lists of the world's best restaurants.

L'Homme Bleu
55 rue Jean-Pierre Timbaud, 75011, www.restaurant-lhommebleu.fr

The friendly service and the delicious dishes cooked up in the tiny (open) kitchen make this Berber restaurant a popular and reliable choice. Slightly unusually for such a restaurant, it also offers a large and surprising choice of cocktails.

Chinatown
avenue de Choisy and avenue d'Ivry, 75013

The 13th arrondissement, around the place d'Italie, became home to Paris's third (and largest) Asian community in the 1970s, making the area a fascinating place to visit – and to eat. If the tower-block architecture is not to everyone's taste, the numerous restaurants cater for all possible preferences.

Maison de l'Aubrac
37 rue Marbeuf, 75008, www.maison-aubrac.com

The owners are also cattle-breeders (in the Aubrac region of France), meaning that you can be absolutely sure of the quality of their steaks. Taking that traceability one step further, racks of meat can be seen maturing in large chilled cabinets inside the restaurant.

Arpège
84 rue de Varenne, 75007, www.alain-passard.com

It may be one of the most expensive restaurants in the city, but Alain Passard's Left Bank temple to good, healthy food should be a once-in-a-lifetime experience for everyone. A specialist in vegetables, Passard uses only produce from his own garden.

Le Griffonnier
8 rue des Saussaies, 75008

This archetypal classic French bistro joyously serves up all the standards, including celery in rib-hugging rémoulade, tripe stew and butter-fried meats smothered with peppery sauces.

Café de la Nouvelle Mairie
19 rue des Fossés Saint-Jacques, 75005

Stylish and bright restaurant offering simple and tasty bistro dishes with a twist, as well as an old-fashioned Latin Quarter atmosphere. The wide selection of natural wines, often at extremely reasonable prices, also helps to bring in the crowds.

Terroir Parisien
20 rue Saint-Victor, 75005, www.yannick-alleno.com/carnet/terroir-parisien

The concept of this restaurant, which has another branch in the Palais Brongniart, the city's old stock exchange, is to use only produce that can be obtained in the Paris area. It is reasonably priced, especially for a concept overseen by the three-star chef Yannick Alléno.

L'Avant Comptoir
3 carrefour de l'Odéon, 75006

Freshly sliced ham, glasses of wine and shoulder-to-shoulder bonhomie are the speciality of this tiny Left Bank institution, which offers an atmosphere more akin to a bar in southwestern France after a rugby match.

BARS AND CAFES

La Caravane
35 rue de la Fontaine au Roi, 75011, www.lacaravane.eu

Now firmly installed as a local favourite, this friendly bric-a-brac-styled bar covers everything from a chilled aperitif to thumping DJ sets. In between, the cheap drinks and hearty Franco-Asian food ensure that the place is permanently busy.

La Maison Pigalle
22 boulevard de Clichy, 75018, www.maison-pigalle.com

This plush and cosy first-floor space, all purple velvet and dimmed lights, hosts regular burlesque events.

HolyBelly
19 rue Lucien Sampaix, 75010, www.holybel.ly

Paris may be a city of cafés, but it has long had a pretty poor reputation for the coffee they serve. A new generation of establishments is changing that, and this intimate and friendly Canal Saint-Martin café is a great example. Its coffee is from the Brulerie de Belleville, a Paris-based importer and roaster.

La Fine Mousse
6 avenue Jean Aicard, 75011, www.lafinemousse.fr

The best place to taste the city's new brews is this bar, which typically has about half a dozen local beers on tap at any one time. The bar itself serves hams and cheeses, but its restaurant opposite offers dishes that are designed to accompany the various beers.

Gossima
4 rue Victor Gelez, 75011, www.gossima.fr

The city's first ping-pong bar! Quiet and family-orientated on weekend afternoons, in the evenings it hosts mini-tournaments in semi-darkness (with luminous ping-pong balls) to a thumping musical soundtrack.

Prescription Cocktail Club
23 rue Mazarine, 75006, www.prescriptioncocktailclub.com

Chic in Paris today means sipping carefully crafted cocktails in underground bars designed to feel like Prohibition-era hideouts. This one offers excellent cocktails – at Parisian prices – and a cosy, relaxed atmosphere.

Les Caves de Prague
8 rue de Prague, 75012, www.facebook.com/cavesdeprague

Despite its bright purple facade, this *bar à vins* remains more discreet than the nearby Baron Rouge, an institution on the edge of the Aligre market that sells wine direct from huge vats. The Prague's young and extremely helpful owner comes from a wine-growing family and favours natural wines.

Acide
24 rue des Moines, 75017, www.acidemacaron.com

The pastry chef Jonathan Blot's *salon de thé* veers more towards the eccentric than the elegant, with curious (and frankly a little uncomfortable) chairs and teapot lampshades, but the delicious cakes and excellent teas are universally popular.

La Dame de Canton
port de la Gare, 75013, www.damedecanton.com

In a tightly packed and heavily populated city, the best place to party today, without disturbing the neighbours, is by – or even on – the river. Most surprising of the numerous floating bars and clubs to the east of the centre is this Chinese junk, which hosts regular concerts (but no longer sails).

Le Dernier Bar avant la Fin du Monde
19 avenue Victoria, 75001, www.dernierbar.com

A self-proclaimed geek bar, this large, very central establishment is aimed primarily at sci-fi fans and gamers, and holds regular events, competitions and concerts. The very reasonable menu and drinks selection attract a wider crowd.

SHOPS

Colette
213 rue Saint-Honoré, 75001, www.colette.fr

This shamelessly snobbish concept store attracts fashion victims from across the world in search of ultra-limited-edition trainers or one-shot collaborations with leading brands.

Grands Magasins
boulevard Haussmann, 75009

Neighbours and rivals for more a than hundred years, the Printemps and Galeries Lafayette stores make for an impressive visit – even for those who hate shopping – right up to the rooftop terraces.

Marché aux Puces du Saint-Ouen
Saint-Ouen, 75018, www.marcheauxpuces-saintouen.com

It may now be very difficult to come away with a bargain from what has become the largest flea market in the world, but that hardly seems to be the point any more. The bazaar today boasts a Philippe Starck-designed restaurant (Ma Cocotte) and a recently-opened 350-room 'zen and organic' hotel called MOB.

Shakespeare & Co.
37 rue de la Bûcherie, 75005, www.shakespeareandcompany.com

The city's most famous English-language bookshop continues to attract and welcome clients from across the city – and the world. The brand now also includes a café next door, offering healthy snacks at reasonable prices (for the district), and decent coffee.

Merci
111 boulevard Beaumarchais, 75003, www.merci-merci.com

The laudable 'concept' of this chic shop is that it donates 100 per cent of its profits to good causes in Madagascar. Housed in a large semi-industrial space that also contains three cafés, the shop concentrates mostly on designer objects and gadgets for the home.

Les Passages
between the Grands Boulevards and the Palais-Royal, 75009/75002

Paris once counted 150 covered arcades, and those that remain provide an off-kilter experience. Try the fashionable passage du Grand-Cerf for design and jewellery, the passage des Panoramas for gastronomy, Galerie Vivienne for its dishevelled elegance, or the surprising passage Brady for Indian restaurants.

Le Bon Marché
24 rue de Sèvres, 75007, www.lebonmarche.com

The oldest and most chic of all Paris department stores, as well as the largest on the Left Bank. A separate building houses a famous food hall that sells everything from caviar to Brazilian black beans.

La Boutique des Inventions
13 rue Saint-Paul, 75004, www.la-boutique-des-inventions.fr

This shop acts as a kind of testing ground for prototypes, where inventors can gauge interest in their designs before moving (with a little luck) into production. Typical items include handy gadgets, household objects and games.

Marché Saint-Quentin
85 bis boulevard de Magenta, 75010

Opened in 1866, this glass, steel and brick building offers possibly the most authentic covered-market experience in Paris. It is within a few minutes' walk of the Gare du Nord.

Le Bonbon au Palais
19 rue Monge, 75005, www.bonbonsaupalais.fr

With decor that resembles a vintage French classroom, this upscale sweet shop sells only French produce, displayed temptingly in large apothecary jars. The friendly owner will point out for you on a large map of France where each confection comes from.

Chronology

4500 BC
A Neolithic fishing community sets up camp by the River Seine, leaving some traces, including pirogue boats.

300 BC
A Celtic tribe known as the Parisii relocates from beyond the Danube and sets up an *oppidum* on an island in the Seine. The exact location of this settlement, which they name Lutetia, is still disputed.

52 BC
The Battle of Lutetia pits the invading Roman army against the Parisii. The Parisii are defeated, but a scorched-earth policy instigated by their leader, Camulogene, means that the Romans inherit an *oppidum* in ruins.

AD 100
Living in tranquillity under the Pax Romana, the Romans and the Parisii build a new city on a Roman model, complete with a forum, an arena and several baths.

360
The Roman leader Julian is proclaimed emperor by his army in Lutetia, giving the city a previously undreamed-of importance.

451
After the Romans depart, Paris is under constant danger of attack. Geneviève, later to become the city's most important patron saint, is said to perform a miracle by encouraging Parisians not

to abandon the city under imminent threat from the army of Attila the Hun. As she promised, Attila does not attack the city.

481

Clovis becomes king of the Franks, and sets up a base in Paris. For the first time Paris is the capital of a unified kingdom. Clovis is later baptized, and becomes the first Christian leader of France.

754

Pepin is crowned king in Saint-Denis, bringing an end to the reign of the Merovingians. The Carolingians subsequently base most of their courts outside Paris, which consequently declines in size and importance.

845–86

Paris suffers a wave of attacks from invading Norman and Viking armies. The brave defence shown by Eudes, the Count of Paris, brings the city back into regional focus and demonstrates the inefficiency of the Carolingians.

987

Hugh Capet, a great-nephew of Eudes, is proclaimed king, bringing an end to the Carolingian dynasty. The Capetians go on to rule through direct line until 1328, and by branches until the end of the French monarchy in 1848.

1079

Birth of Pierre Abélard, one of the most famous Parisian lovers, thanks to his tragic, lifelong affair with Héloïse. Abélard is also one of the city's great teachers, and helps to build the city's international academic renown, notably in the new 'Latin Quarter' on the city's Left Bank.

1137

Louis VII, one of history's losers, is crowned king. Despite losing a wife, several battles and half the kingdom during his reign, he nevertheless – with the powerful and influential Abbot Suger – helps to introduce Gothic architecture, notably with

the new church at Saint-Denis and with Notre-Dame on the
Île de la Cité.

1180

Philippe II (Auguste) is crowned king of France. Over his 43-year
reign he transforms the capital, notably by building an enormous
protective wall around the city, incorporating the first Louvre.
Through numerous successful battles, Philippe also greatly increases
the size and importance of France, and firmly establishes Paris as its
religious, academic, administrative and financial capital.

1242–8

The immensely pious Louis IX, later St Louis, builds the Sainte-
Chapelle beside the royal palace to house the relics he has purchased at astronomical prices. Academia in the city increases even
more in importance with the creation of the Sorbonne university.

1314

The leader of the Knights Templar, Jacques de Molay, is burned
at the stake in front of Notre-Dame after refusing to accept the
trumped-up charges of Philippe IV (le Bel). Before dying, de Molay
declares a curse on the puppet pope installed by Philippe, and on
the Capetian dynasty. The pope suffers a quick death, and within
fourteen years three kings also die without producing any heirs.

1337

The beginning of the Hundred Years War, which famously lasts for
114 years. Paris suffers terribly during this period, through conflict,
civil war and the Black Death. It even suffers the ignominy of being
run by an Englishman, the Duke of Bedford, for fifteen years.

1429

Joan of Arc is injured when leading an unsuccessful assault on
Paris. Two years later she is burned at the stake in Rouen.

1515

Coronation of François 1, who is nearly 2 m (6 1/2 ft) tall and 'every
inch the Renaissance king'. He brings Italian artists, including

Leonardo da Vinci, to France, but prefers to spend his time in the relaxed royal chateaux on the Loire, rather than in Paris.

1572

In the so-called St Bartholomew's Day massacre on 24 August, as many as 15,000 Protestants are killed across France, mostly in Paris. The massacre is said to have begun after the bells were rung at the church of Saint-Germain l'Auxerrois, opposite the Louvre. Future ruler Henri of Navarre, in Paris for his wedding, narrowly escapes death.

1604

After laying siege to Paris for five years, the former Protestant Henri IV is finally crowned king. His claim to the throne is accepted only after he has converted to Catholicism at Saint-Denis in 1593. Henri's reign, although at sixteen years not particularly long, is one of the most productive in the history of Paris, notably including the completion of the pont Neuf and the construction of the place Royale (des Vosges) and place Dauphine.

1610

Following Henri IV's assassination by François Ravaillac, Louis XIII ascends the throne aged only eight. His reign is marked by the building of the Île Saint-Louis and the Palais-Royal, the latter of which becomes the home of his influential first minister, Cardinal Richelieu.

1643

Louis XIV arrives on the throne, aged only three.

1648–53

A period of civil war known as the Fronde impels Louis and his regent mother, Anne of Austria, to quit Paris temporarily. Although just a child during these two major uprisings, Louis develops a lifelong distrust of Paris as a result.

1682

Louis XIV abandons Paris for his colossal new chateau in Versailles, taking the entire royal court with him. Paris, though, keeps an administrative role, and continues to grow in size and population notably with Les Invalides, the place des Victoires and the place Vendôme. Since France is considered impossible to invade, Louis pulls down the city walls and replaces them with a planted promenade.

1770

Following the largely tactical marriage of fifteen-year-old Louis (later Louis XVI) to fourteen-year-old Marie Antoinette of Austria, a celebratory firework display at the place de la Concorde ends in disaster and the deaths of 132 people.

1789

Suffering under the effects of crushing debts, political instability and weak leadership, Paris slips into revolution. Louis XVI and Marie Antoinette are taken at Versailles and forced to live under house arrest at the Tuileries palace. After a miscalculated escape attempt, the revolutionary authorities vote to execute the king and queen. Both are beheaded in 1793, and the country subsequently slides into a murderous and chaotic period known as the Terror, which ends a year later with the execution of Robespierre.

1799

With Royalists pushing to make a comeback during the feeble and corrupt Directory government, a general named Napoléon Bonaparte organizes the Coup du 18 brumaire and takes control of the country on 9 November.

1804

After leading French forces to spectacular military victories in Italy and Egypt, Napoléon returns to Paris and crowns himself emperor at Notre-Dame. Declaring his desire to make Paris the greatest city in Europe, he launches a number of major projects, few of which will be completed in his lifetime. His longest-lasting achievements are the creation of a new civil code, much of which is still in place today; the transformation of the Louvre; and the building and installation of new sources of water for the capital.

1814–15

After further military success in Austria, Napoléon overreaches himself in Russia and suffers a crushing defeat at the Battle of the Nations in Leipzig. The victorious Allied forces march on Paris, arriving in the city in March 1815. Napoléon is banished to Elba, and the Bourbons and Louis XVIII return to take control. Napoléon quickly escapes, and returns to Paris to chase off Louis. It proves a short-lived comeback, and ends in catastrophic failure at the Battle of Waterloo. When Napoléon is banished for good to the unescapable island of St Helena, Louis returns safely to the throne.

1824

Obese and bedridden, Louis XVIII becomes the last French king to die during his reign. He is replaced by his brother, the last grandson of Louis XV, Charles X, who is already seventy years old.

1830

Paris overthrows another king when it rises up during the *Trois Glorieuses*. The authoritarian Charles is suspected of wanting a return to absolute monarchy, and protests from a small group of young men quickly escalate into a full-blown revolution. After declaring that he can 'see no middle way between the throne and the scaffold', Charles nevertheless escapes, leaving Louis-Philippe to take over as the 'July monarchy'.

1848

After nearly 1,500 years, the French monarchy finally comes to an end, once again after a revolution in Paris. The country's experiment with a constitutional monarchy had shown its limits when Louis-Philippe refused further reform. Confronted by a rebellion, the king abdicates and escapes to England as 'Mr Smith'.

1851

Napoléon's nephew Louis-Napoléon Bonaparte, a surprising president of the Second Republic, surprises even more people by organizing a *coup d'état* to coincide with the anniversary of both the Battle of Austerlitz and his uncle's coronation. With his imposed term as president approaching its end, he chooses to create a Second Empire (and declare himself Napoléon III), a move that immediately receives strong public support.

1870

After transforming the centre of Paris to an unprecedented extent in collaboration with his loyal prefect, Georges-Eugène Haussmann, Napoléon III begins to look outside France to cement his place in posterity. His attack on Prussia gets no further than the eastern city of Sedan, where he is captured. Prussian forces then march towards Paris and lay siege to the city.

1871

Following a terrible five-month siege over one of the coldest winters in recent history, the French army signs an armistice with the Prussians. As part of the agreement, the Prussian army is allowed to parade through the centre of Paris. Humiliated by this affront, and determined to keep up the fight, Paris declares an independent government called the Commune. A second ten-week siege begins, the city this time surrounded by French forces. The movement ends in fire and slaughter; many buildings are destroyed and over 20,000 communards executed or banished.

1875

A one-vote majority is enough to signal the beginning of the Third Republic. Although never stable, it will last for more than seventy years. The French government, however, remains in Versailles until 1879.

1878

Determined to show that the country has recovered from recent conflicts, Paris organizes a 'sober' Universal Exhibition focusing mostly on industry.

1885

Two million people line the streets of Paris to watch the body of Victor Hugo wend its way to the Panthéon. The death of Hugo –

who was as old as the century itself – marks the end of Romanticism and a move towards the modernity and realism of Émile Zola and the Impressionist painters.

1889

For Paris's fourth Universal Exhibition (after 1855, 1867 and 1878), the city unveils the tallest building in the world, the Eiffel Tower. Over 32 million people visit the exhibition.

1900

Now firmly installed as the world's leading host, Paris welcomes over 50 million visitors to what is perhaps the most spectacular Universal Exhibition of all. Based around the Alexandre III bridge and the new Grand and Petit Palais, the exhibition largely overlooks industry in favour of art and commerce. To move visitors around, Paris opens its first Métro line.

1910

During the worst floods for 150 years, much of the centre of Paris is submerged by the overflowing Seine.

1914

The Socialist leader Jean Jaurès, France's last hope for a negotiated solution with Germany, is assassinated in a café on 31 July. Three days later France is at war. Paris quickly empties as a generation of young men are sent out to the front. General Joseph Gallieni, who is left behind by the French government to defend Paris against a seemingly inevitable invasion it had little hope of fending off, nevertheless helps to push the German army back during the Battle of the Marne.

1918

Despite being the closest major city to the conflict, Paris suffers very little physical damage from the slaughter taking place on its doorstep. Only 266 Parisians die as a result of bomb attacks during the war, but as the conflict ends, Spanish influenza begins killing three hundred people a day in Paris alone.

1925

The *années folles* are lit up by the International Exhibition of Modern Decorative and Industrial Arts. The city is confirmed as a world capital of pleasure, art and consumer culture.

1931

With France's influence over its colonies beginning to wane, Paris nevertheless hosts a spectacular – but controversial – Colonial Exhibition.

1937

A final Universal Exhibition, aiming to highlight France's international importance, instead highlights growing tension across Europe, notably between Germany and Russia.

1940

After a 'phoney war' lasting nearly a year, Paris is occupied by the German army. A week later Adolf Hitler makes his first and last visit to the city. The early-morning tour takes in the Opéra, the Trocadéro, Sacré-Coeur and – most significantly of all for Hitler – Napoléon's tomb in Les Invalides.

1942

The first *rafles* round up a large proportion of the city's Jewish community. During the war, over 76,000 people are deported from France; fewer than 3,000 return.

1944

General Leclerc's troops liberate Paris on 24 August, narrowly in front of the u.s. Army's 4th division. Two days later General de Gaulle walks in triumph – and no little personal danger – down the Champs-Élysées.

1945

A Fourth Republic is voted in, but de Gaulle, tired of the squabbling and the 'absurd ballet', retires from public life.

1954

The coldest winter in living memory kills dozens of homeless and poorly housed people, drawing attention to the terrible state of most buildings in Paris and the surrounding area.

1958

Charles de Gaulle returns, and helps to create a Fifth Republic with increased powers for the president.

1961–2

With the Algerian War dragging on for a seventh year, the conflict is also exported to Paris. Protests by the city's Algerian community against curfews are put down savagely by the police. Dozens of protesters are killed and thrown into the Seine. As the conflict draws to a close, splinter groups with links to the French army who want to keep Algeria under French control make an attempt on de Gaulle's life.

1968

In May, a student protest in Nanterre spills over into Paris and the rest of the country, and almost succeeds in toppling the government. Although France is experiencing an extremely strong period of growth and wealth, its bourgeois conservatism no longer corresponds with the aspirations of the younger generation.

1969

Charles de Gaulle resigns from office after losing a referendum. Retiring again from public life, he dies a year later. He is replaced as president by Georges Pompidou, who seeks to modernize Paris by easing access for cars and increasing the height of new buildings.

1976

Jacques Chirac is elected the thirteenth mayor of Paris, and the first since 1871.

1981

François Mitterrand becomes the first Socialist president of France since Vincent Auriol at the beginning of the 1950s. His two terms in office over fourteen years are marked by nine *grands projets* for Paris, including the Opéra Bastille and the pyramid at the Louvre.

1995

Jacques Chirac becomes president of the French Republic.

2001

After 25 years of right-wing dominance, Paris elects a Socialist mayor. Bertrand Delanoë is also the first openly homosexual mayor of a major international city.

2005

France discovers the extent of the social problems in its suburbs after riots break out in the Parisian suburb of Clichy-sous-Bois following the accidental deaths of two young inhabitants. The riots spread across the Paris region and the rest of France.

2008

Delanoë is re-elected as mayor of Paris with an increased majority.

2014

The Socialists retain control of Paris, this time under the city's first female mayor, Anne Hidalgo.

2015

In January, seventeen people are killed in two separate terrorist attacks in Paris. The perpetrators of the attack on the offices of the satirical newspaper *Charlie Hebdo*, Chérif and Saïd Kouachi, had been born, brought up and radicalized in Paris. A further 130 people are killed in a second wave of attacks in November.

2016

The Métropole du Grand Paris, a new legal structure grouping Paris with 124 surrounding towns, is created on 1 January. The new entity will have responsibility for around seven million people, and control urban planning and social, economic and cultural development.

References

p. 16 Quoted in Eric Hazan, *L'Invention de Paris* (Paris, 2002), p. 83.

p. 16 Quoted in Comte Fleury and Louis Sonolet, *La Société du Second Empire, 1863–1867* (1928), available at www.archive.org.

p. 16 Quoted in Emmanuel-Auguste-Dieudonné, Comte de Las Cases, *Mémorial de Sainte Hélène: Journal of the Private Life and Conversations of the Emperor Napoleon at Saint Helena* (London, 1823), available at www.archive.org.

p. 16 From a speech made by Louis-Napoléon Bonaparte at a banquet at the Hôtel de Ville, 10 December 1850.

p. 16 Eric Hazan, *Paris sous tension* (Paris, 2001), p. 11.

p. 17 Ibid., p. 14.

p. 17 Gabriel Hanotaux, *La Seine et les quais* (Paris, 1901), p. 12.

p. 17 Jules Romains, *Puissances de Paris* (Paris, 1919), p. 125.

p. 17 Quoted in Colin Jones, *Paris: Biography of a City* (London, 2004), p. xvi.

p. 22 Julius Caesar, *De bello gallico*, trans. W. A. MacDevitt (London, 1929), available at www.gutenberg.org.

p. 23 *The Roman History of Ammianus Marcellinus*, trans. C. D. Yonge (London, 1894), available at www.archive.org.

p. 27 *The Works of the Emperor Julian*, vol. II, trans. Wilmer Cave Wright (Cambridge, MA, 1913), available at www.gutenberg.org.

p. 30 Quotations from Colin Jones, 'Theodore Vacquer and the Archaeology of Modernity in Haussmann's Paris', *Transactions of the Royal Historical Society*, XVII (December 2007), pp. 157–83.

p. 33 Bruno Dumézil, *Des Gaulois aux Carolingiens* (Paris, 2013), p. 73.

p. 33 Quoted in Philippe Delay, *De Lutèce à Paris* (Paris, 1992), p. 86.

p. 36   Quotations from Abbon de Saint-Germain-des-Près, *Le Siège de Paris par les Normands, 885–892* (Clermont-Ferrand, 2010), pp. 21, 26, 22, 35, 83, 11.

p. 42   *Lettres d'Abélard et d'Héloïse* (Paris, 1875), available at www.wikisource.org.

p. 47   Quoted in Alistair Horne, *Seven Ages of Paris* (London, 2002), p. 21.

p. 48   Urban Tigner Holmes, *Daily Living in the Twelfth Century: Based on the Observations of Alexander Neckham in London and Paris* (Madison, WI, 1952), p. 81.

p. 51   From 'Chronique métrique attribué à Geofroi de Paris', quoted in Alain Demurger, *The Last Templar* (London, 2004), pp. 197–8.

p. 52   Quotations from Henri Scepi, *Henri Scepi commente Notre-Dame de Paris de Victor Hugo* (Paris, 2006).

p. 55   Quoted in Horne, *Seven Ages of Paris*, p. 74.

p. 60   Quoted in Joan DeJean, *How Paris Became Paris: The Invention of the Modern City* (New York, 2014), p. 6.

p. 60   Jones, *Paris: Biography of a City*, p. 158.

p. 61   Quoted in Hazan, *L'Invention de Paris*, p. 83.

p. 61   Quoted in DeJean, *How Paris Became Paris*, p. 6.

p. 61   Ibid., p. 50.

p. 65   Website of the Académie française: www.academie-francaise.fr.

p. 65   The decree was the Ordinance of Villers-Cotterêts (1539).

p. 65   Georges Bernanos, *Correspondance inédite, 1904–1948* (Paris, 1983), p. 124.

p. 66   Quoted in Benjamin Arranger, ed., *Paris vu par les écrivains* (Paris, 2003), p. 79.

p. 68   'a king whose name is already enough to fill the universe'; Jean Racine, 'La Nymphe de la Seine' (1660).

p. 68   Quoted in Horne, *Seven Ages of Paris*, p. 123.

p. 70   DeJean, *How Paris Became Paris*, p. 156.

p. 71   Nancy Mitford, *The Sun King* (London, 2011), p. 48.

p. 71   Quoted ibid., p. 96.

p. 71   Quoted in Voltaire, *Le Siècle de Louis XIV* (Paris, 1751), available at www.gallica.bnf.fr.

p. 72   Pierre de Marivaux, *Lettres sur les habitants de Paris* [1717–18] (Paris, 2002), p. 21.

p. 72   Ibid., p. 45.

p. 75 Quoted in Graham Robb, *Parisians: An Adventure History of Paris* (London, 2010), p. 15.

p. 75 Bernard Marchand, *Paris: Histoire d'une ville, XIX–XXème siècle* (Paris, 1993), p. 42.

p. 76 Jacques-Antoine Dulaure, *Histoire physique, civile et morale de Paris: Depuis les premiers temps historiques jusqu'à nos jours* (Paris, 1826), available at www.gallica.bnf.fr.

p. 78 Quoted in Arranger, *Paris vu par les écrivains*, p. 217.

p. 79 Voltaire, *Le Siècle de Louis XIV*.

p. 79 Quoted in Horne, *Seven Ages of Paris*, p. 176.

p. 80 David P. Jordan, *The King's Trial: The French Revolution vs. Louis XVI* (Oakland, CA, 1979), p. 66.

p. 82 Quoted in Antonia Fraser, *Marie Antoinette* (London, 2001), p. 420.

p. 83 Quoted in Jones, *Paris: Biography of a City*, p. 289.

p. 83 Charles Saunier, *Les Conquêtes artistiques de la Révolution et de l'Empire: Reprises et abandons des alliés en 1815, leurs conséquences sur les musées d'Europe* (Paris, 1902), available at www.gallica.bnf.fr.

p. 85 Quoted in Horne, *Seven Ages of Paris*, p. 236.

p. 85 Quoted in Alain Rustenholz, *Paris des avant-gardes* (Paris, 2004), p. 34.

p. 87 Louis-Sébastien Mercier, *Le Nouveau Paris* (Paris, 1994), p. 338.

p. 87 Ibid.

p. 88 Honoré de Balzac, *Facino Cane* [1837], trans. Clara Bell (1999), available at www.gutenberg.org.

p. 91 Message published in *Le Constitutionnel* newspaper, 3 December 1851.

p. 91 Quoted in Jones, *Paris: Biography of a City*, p. 352.

p. 91 Georges Eugène Haussmann, *Baron Haussmann: Mémoires*, ed. Françoise Choay (Paris, 2000), p. 790.

p. 92 Quoted in Hazan, *L'Invention de Paris*, p. 28.

p. 92 Victor Fournel, *Paris nouveau et Paris futur* (Paris, 1865), available at www.gallica.bnf.fr.

p. 94 Quoted in Robb, *Parisians*, p. 138.

p. 94 Patrice de Moncan, *Paris avant/après* (Paris, 2010), p. 13.

p. 97 Quotations from George Valance, *Haussmann le grand* (Paris, 2000), p. 284.

p. 98   Quoted in Horne, *Seven Ages of Paris*, p. 286.

p. 99   Quotations from Prosper-Olivier Lissagaray, *History of the Paris Commune* [1886], trans. Eleanor Marx (Cambridge, MA, 2011), e-book.

p. 103   Quoted in Joanna Richardson, *Paris Under Siege* (London, 1982), p. 186.

p. 106   Geoffrey Wawro, *The Franco–Prussian War: The German Conquest of France in 1870–1871* (Cambridge, 2005), p. 305.

p. 106   Jones, *Paris: Biography of a City*, p. 382.

p. 107   Louis Leroy, writing in *Le Charivari* (25 April 1874).

p. 108   Émile Zola, *La Bête Humaine*, trans. Ernest Alfred Vizetelly (London, 1901), available at www.archive.org.

p. 108   Robert Abirached, preface to Émile Zola, *Le Ventre de Paris* (Paris, 1997), e-book.

p. 109   Ibid.

p. 109   'Les Artistes contre la tour Eiffel', *Le Temps* (14 February 1887).

p. 109   Ibid.

p. 109   W. Scott Haine, *The World of the Paris Café: Sociability among the French Working Class, 1789–1914* (Baltimore, MD, 1996), p. 3.

p. 111   Joris-Karl Huysmans, *Paris et autres textes* (Paris, 2015), pp. 11–12.

p. 111   Pierre Drachline and Claude-Castelli, 'Casque d'or et les apaches', *Renaudot et Cie* (Paris, 1990), p. 38.

p. 111   Quoted in Haine, *The World of the Paris Café*, p. 5.

p. 111   Weber, quoted in Judith Thurman, *A Life of Colette* (London, 2000), p. 82; Blum, quoted in Horne, *Seven Ages of Paris*, p. 325.

p. 111   Quoted in Kate Cambor, *Gilded Youth: Three Lives in France's Belle Époque* (New York, 2009), p. 57.

p. 112   'Les Artistes contre la tour Eiffel'.

p. 112   Quoted in *Le Temps* (14 February 1887).

p. 115   Thurman, *A Life of Colette*, p. 87.

p. 117   Léon-Paul Fargue, *Le Piéton de Paris* (Paris, 1998), p. 172.

p. 118   Charles Péguy, *L'Argent* (Paris, 2013), e-book.

p. 120   Daniel Halévy, *Pays parisiens* (Paris, 1932), p. 218.

p. 120   Quoted in Horne, *Seven Ages of Paris*, p. 351.

p. 121   Thurman, *A Life of Colette*, p. 260.

p. 121   Quoted in Horne, *Seven Ages of Paris*, p. 359.

p. 121   Quoted in John Baxter, *Paris at the End of the World* (Sydney, 2014), e-book.

p. 124   Quoted in Jones, *Paris: Biography of a City*, p. 440.

p. 125   Henry Miller, *Tropic of Cancer* (1934), chap. 8.

p. 126   Fargue, *Le Piéton de Paris*, p. 140.

p. 126   André Warnod, *Les Plaisirs de la rue* (1920), quoted in Arranger, *Paris vu par les écrivains*, p. 323.

p. 129   Quoted in Horne, *Seven Ages of Paris*, p. 390.

p. 131   Quoted ibid., p. 396.

p. 131   All quotations about the visit of Hitler to Paris are from Robb, *Parisians*.

p. 132   Jean Guéhenno, *Journal des années noires* (Paris, 1947), 7 September 1940 and 14 June 1941.

p. 132   Quoted in Thurman, *A Life of Colette*, p. 442.

p. 134   Quoted in Horne, *Seven Ages of Paris*, p. 419.

p. 134   Quoted in Jones, *Paris: Biography of a City*, p. 489.

p. 135   Quoted in Horne, *Seven Ages of Paris*, p. 429.

p. 137   *Le Petit Parisien* (5 December 1937).

p. 137   Boris Vian, *Manuel de Saint-Germain-des-Prés* (Paris, 2001).

p. 138   Hazan, *Paris sous tension*, p. 88.

p. 139   Ibid., p. 89.

p. 138   Quoted in Horne, *Seven Ages of Paris*, p. 429.

p. 141   Quoted in Christine Faure, *Mai 68: Jour et nuit* (Paris, 1998), p. 31.

p. 142   Quoted in Hazan, *L'Invention de Paris*, p. 405.

p. 142   Quoted in Laurent Joffrin, *Mai 68: Une Historie de mouvement* (Paris, 1988), p. 51.

p. 142   Quoted ibid., p. 68.

p. 143   Ibid., p. 35.

p. 143   Quoted in Robb, *Parisians*, p. 364.

p. 145   Ibid., p. 386.

p. 145   Quoted in Jones, *Paris: Biography of a City*, p. 489.

p. 147   Quotations taken from the artist's official website: http://pignon-ernest.com.

p. 148   Quoted in Yvan Combeau, *Histoire de Paris* (Paris, 1999), p. 117.

p. 150   Quoted in Simon Kuper, 'Les Illusions perdues des "Black-Blanc-Beur"', *Courier International* (2 July 2008).

p. 151 Jules Verne, *Paris au xxème siècle* (Paris, 1994), p. 168.

p. 152 Philippe Subra, *Le Grand Paris: Géopolitique d'une ville mondiale* (Paris, 2012), p. 243.

p. 154 Jones, *Paris: Biography of a City*, p. 544.

p. 155 Lauren Houssin, 'Antoine Grumbach: "La Seine est le vecteur d'identité de la métropole"', www.liberation.fr, 11 December 2014.

p. 156 Paris opposition member Philippe Goujon, quoted in Bertrand Gréco, 'Paris: Le Bilan de dix ans de Delanoë', www.lejdd.fr, 17 March 2011.

p. 157 'AFP', 'Avec ses Tours, Delanoë marche sur des oeufs', *L'Express* (8 July 2008), www.lexpress.fr.

p. 160 François Maspero, *Les Passagers du Roissy-express* (Paris, 1990), p. 25.

p. 161 Halévy, *Pays parisiens*, p. 159.

p. 163 Geoffroy Clavel, 'Comment l'architecte de la nouvelle place de la République juge-t-il Nuit debout?', *Le Huffington Post* (13 April 2016), www.huffingtonpost.fr.

p. 163 Quoted in Anne-Charlotte Dusseaulx, 'Pourquoi la place de la République est "l'espace de tous les possibles"', *Le Journal du Dimanche* (14 April 2016).

p. 169 Alain Beuve-Méry, 'Le Cinéma français va bien, merci!', *Le Monde Économie* (6 May 2015), www.lemonde.fr.

p. 174 *Le Figaro* (8 May 1931).

p. 175 *L'Humanité* (8 May 1931).

p. 176 Former minister and museum instigator Jacques Toubon; quotation displayed on an information panel inside the museum.

p. 176 Maureen Murphy, *Un Palais pour une Cité. Du Musée des Colonies à la Cité Nationale de l'Histoire de l'Immigration* (Paris, 2007), p. 60.

p. 176 Jones, *Paris: Biography of a City*, p. 469.

p. 177 Daniel Roche, *Le Peuple de Paris* (Paris, 1981), p. 32.

p. 177 Halévy, *Pays parisiens*, p. 9.

p. 181 François-Régis Gaudry, '"La Jeune Rue" dans le Marais, le projet gastronomique et design qui va changer Paris', *L'Express* (25 March 2014), www.lexpress.fr.

p. 182 Zola, *Le Ventre de Paris*, p. 245.

p. 182 Letter from Victor Hugo to Romain Boulanger, 24 September 1880.

p. 183 A. A. Gill, 'Tour de Gall', *Vanity Fair* (3 March 2011), www.vanityfair.com.

p. 183 Ibid.

p. 183 Michael Steinberger, 'Can Anyone Save French Food?', *New York Times* (28 March 2014), www.nytimes.com.

p. 184 Quotations from Patrick Rambourg, *Histoire de la cuisine et de la gastronomie françaises* (Paris, 2010).

p. 186 Adam Gopnik, 'No Rules!', *New Yorker* (5 April 2010), www.newyorker.com.

p. 187 Ibid.

p. 188 Ernest Hemingway, *A Moveable Feast* [1964] (London, 2011), p. 31.

p. 189 George Orwell, *Down and Out in Paris and London* [1933] (London, 2003), p. 2.

p. 189 Georges Duhamel, *Confession de minuit* (Paris, 1920).

p. 190 Hemingway, *A Moveable Feast*, p. 15.

p. 192 Jean-Paul Clébert, *Paris insolite* (Paris, 1952), p. 151.

p. 192 Guy de Maupassant, *Les Dimanches d'un bourgeois de Paris* (Paris, 2004), p. 18.

p. 193 Robert Beck, *Histoire du Dimanche, de 1700 à nos jours* (Ivry, 1997), p. 197.

p. 193 Quoted ibid., p. 361.

p. 201 Simone Delattre, *Les douze heures noires: La nuit à Paris au XIXe siècle* (Paris, 2000), p. 34.

p. 201 Quotations from Rétif de la Bretonne, *Les Nuits de Paris* (Paris, 1986), p. 218.

p. 204 Alfred Delvau, *Les Heures Parisiennes* (Paris, 1866), available at www.gallica.bnf.fr.

p. 205 J. de Neuville, Delattre, *Les douze heures noires*, p. 122.

p. 205 Géraldine Sarratia and Fabien Cante, 'Quand la Nuit parisienne meurt en silence', www.lesinrocks.com, 2 November 2009.

p. 206 Delvau, *Les Heures Parisiennes*.

p. 207 This and subsequent quotations from Louis Aragon, *Le Paysan de Paris* (Paris, 1926), p. 21.

p. 207 Walter Benjamin, *Paris: Capitale du XIXe siècle* (Paris, 2013), p. 14.

p. 207 Aragon, *Le Paysan de Paris*, p. 21.

p. 208   Quoted in Sybil Canac and Bruno Cabanis, *Passages couverts de Paris* (Issy-les-Moulineaux, 2011), p. 10.

p. 210   Quoted in Marie Ottavi, 'Les Frères Segas: Un festival de cannes', http://next.liberation.fr, 31 January 2014.

p. 211   Germain Bapst, *Histoire des Panoramas* (Paris, 1891), available at www.gallica.bnf.fr.

p. 212   Aragon, *Le Paysan de Paris*, p. 89.

p. 213   *Paris passages*, exh. cat., Espace Fondation EDF (Arles, 2002).

p. 213   Romains, *Puissances de Paris*, p. 90.

p. 213   Honoré de Balzac, *Les Illusions perdues: Un Grand Homme de province à Paris* (1839), available at http://fr.wikisource.org.

p. 214   Quoted in Jean-Claude Delorme and Anne-Marie Dubois, *Passages couverts Parisiens* (Paris, 1996), p. 72.

p. 214   Ibid., p. 64.

p. 215   Quotations from Fargue, *Le Piéton de Paris*, p. 72.

p. 216   Jacques Prévert, 'Chanson de la Seine' (1946).

p. 217   'Under Mirabeau Bridge the river slips away / And lovers / Must I be reminded / Joy came always after pain'. Guillaume Apollinaire, 'Le Pont Mirabeau' (1913). English translation by Donald Revell, from *Alcools: Poems by Guillaume Appollinaire* (Middletown, CT, 1995).

p. 218   Quoted in Joël Schmidt, *Lutèce: Paris, des origines à Clovis* (Paris, 2009), p. 94.

p. 218   Gabriel Hanotaux, *La Seine et les quais: Promenade d'un bibliophile* (Lausanne, 1999), p. 28.

p. 218   Fargue, *Le Piéton de Paris*, p. 73.

p. 219   Ibid., p. 76.

p. 222   Maxime Du Camp, *Paris: Ses Organes, ses fonctions et sa vie dans la seconde moitié du XIXe siècle* (Paris, 1875), available at www.gallica.bnf.fr.

Suggested Reading and Viewing

Books about Paris

Ayers, Andrew, *The Architecture of Paris* (Stuttgart and London, 2004). An incisive dissection of the city's many varied constructions, recounting both story and style. A personal bible.

DeJean, Joan, *How Paris Became Paris: The Invention of the Modern City* (New York, 2014). Sharply and persuasively debunks the notion that Paris is a nineteenth-century city.

Dyer, Geoff, *Paris Trance: A Romance* (Edinburgh, 2012). Paris of the 1990s seen through the eyes of two young couples. A hypnotic and nostalgic tale of music, ecstasy, friendship and self-discovery.

Hazan, Eric, *The Invention of Paris: A History in Footsteps* (London and New York, 2011). An incredibly rich and detailed tour of the city's many layers and identities, by the person who knows Paris best.

Hemingway, Ernest, *A Moveable Feast* (1964). Hemingway's posthumously published memoir is a nostalgic return to his young years as a struggling writer. An enduring Paris classic.

Horne, Alistair, *Seven Ages of Paris* (London, 2002). Elegantly and precisely details seven key periods in the city's history.

Hugo, Victor, *Notre-Dame de Paris* (1831; published in English in 1833 as *The Hunchback of Notre-Dame*). Hugo's epic of the Middle Ages lovingly recreates the era and is deservedly one of the city's most famous tales.

Jones, Colin, *Paris: Biography of a City* (London, 2004). Paris can be proud to have its story told by someone who effortlessly mixes solid research, deft analysis and plenty of humour.

Marchand, Bernard, *Paris: Histoire d'une ville, XIX–XXème siècle* (Paris, 1993). An extremely dense but always readable investigation

of nineteenth- and twentieth-century Paris. Only available in
French.

Orwell, George, *Down and Out in Paris and London* (1933).
Orwell's study may have represented a form of poverty tourism,
but he is a generous and sensitive guide.

Robb, Graham, *Parisians: An Adventure History of Paris* (London,
2010). Tells the history of Paris from the point of view of some of
its well-known – and much lesser-known – actors. A constantly
surprising and engaging read.

Sante, Luc, *The Other Paris* (New York, 2015). A lively, informative
and visually rich tour of the dark side of the City of Light.

Soupault, Philippe, *Last Nights of Paris* (Cambridge, MA, 2008).
A surreal nocturnal ramble through a city peopled by
bookmakers, thieves, prostitutes and murderers. Admirably
translated into English by the poet William Carlos Williams.

Zola, Émile, *The Belly of Paris* (Oxford, 2009). Sometimes translated
as *The Fat and the Thin*, Zola's food novel is perhaps a little
meagre in story, but gorges itself on descriptive detail about the
city's historic market.

Films

Donen, Stanley, *Funny Face* (1959). With both Audrey Hepburn and
the city in vibrant Technicolor, what's not to like? Bonjour Paris!

Kassovitz, Mathieu, *La Haine* (1995). Set mostly in the city's
suburbs and filmed in raw black and white, Kassovitz's splenetic
film marked a generation.

Linklater, Richard, *Before Sunset* (2004). Ten years after their first
meeting in Vienna, a star-crossed couple meet again in Paris.
Their subsequent non-stop talking and walking correspond
perfectly to the city.

Malle, Louis, *Zazie in the Metro* (1960). A ten-year-old girl on a
first trip to Paris is desperate to experience the Métro – only to
discover that the network's staff are on strike. Based on Raymond
Queneau's playful book.

Truffaut, François, *The 400 Blows* (1959). Truffaut's semi-
autobiographical New Wave classic, filmed largely around Pigalle
and Montmartre, is a touching depiction of adolescent angst and
the search for emancipation.

Online

Up-to-date insider guides on where to eat, visit and shop, historical and cultural vignettes, classified ads in English for those staying longer, and an aural visit to many parts of the city.

FUSAC
www.fusac.fr

Girls Guide to Paris
https://girlsguidetoparis.com

Lost in Cheeseland
www.lostincheeseland.com

Paris by Mouth
www.parisbymouth.com

Parisian Fields
https://parisianfields.com

Que Faire à Paris
www.quefaire.paris.fr

Soundlandscapes
www.soundlandscapes.wordpress.com

Spotted by locals
www.spottedbylocals.com/paris

Time Out Paris
www.timeout.com/paris

Acknowledgements

Thanks firstly to everyone who has supported, helped and inspired Invisible Paris over the years. In particular I would like to thank Peter Olson, Des Coulam, Philippa and Norman at Parisian Fields, Cara Black, Robert Wheeler, Joanna Walsh, Bart and Sanne from Spotted by Locals, the team at Atlas Obscura, Jethro Massey, Shane Lynam for his visual inspiration and friendship, and above all Tim Pike, whose contribution has gone as far as helping to shape and correct this book. He has taken the Invisible to Bordeaux with a blog that everyone should discover.

I am extremely grateful also to Vivian Constantinopoulos, my editor at Reaktion Books, who found Invisible Paris and believed in my ability to write this book. The journey has been a long one but she has been an excellent and supportive guide. I extend my thanks to everyone else at Reaktion Books, who have always been efficient, friendly and helpful. Any errors in this book are entirely my responsibility.

I thank all those who helped in the production of the book, especially Sylvanie de Lutece, Jean Mora and Marie-Aude Laurent at Le Meurice, and Virginie Champion and Jean-Jacques Schpoliansky at Le Balzac. A very special mention also to the people of Paris. As I was writing the book, Paris and its inhabitants suffered a number of terrible attacks, but the spirit and defiance they have shown since continues to prove to me that I live in one of the world's great cities.

Immense gratitude always to my family in England for their love and support and for giving me a passion for exploring, learning and sharing. Finally, my biggest thanks of all to my wonderful Paris family, Patricia, Félix and Jeanne. You have always been my inspiration and this book is for you.

Photo Acknowledgements

The author and publishers wish to express their thanks to the below sources of illustrative material and/or permission to reproduce it.

AFP/Getty Images: pp. 142, 148; Alamy/Ian Dagnall: p. 64; courtesy Dorchester Collection: p. 194; Getty Images/Roger-Viollet: pp. 128, 139; iStockphoto: pp. 8 top (Nikada), 8 bottom and 219 (Jacques van Dinteren), 9 top (dennisvdw), 9 bottom (Lembi Buchanan), 10 bottom (Bosca 78), 11 (Anna Bryukhanova), 12 below (Arie J. Jager), 14 (sborisov), 58 (MasterLu), 156 (7000), 157 (IrinaSafronova), 162 (Cloud-Mine-Amsterdam), 219 (Jacques van Dinteren); Library of Congress, Washington, DC: pp. 18, 93, 110 (top and bottom), 115, 119, 124, 126, 127, 133; MANCIE/SIPA/Rex Features/Shutterstock: p. 138; Ernest Pignon: p. 146; Adam Roberts: pp. 6, 7 (top), 10 (top), 12 (bottom), 13, 24, 25, 26, 32, 40, 45, 62, 63, 86, 113, 122, 145, 164, 166, 168, 169, 170, 172, 177, 178, 186, 190, 191, 202, 203, 209, 211, 221, 222, 224; Roger-Viollet/Rex Features/Shutterstock: pp. 31, 130; Tangopaso: p. 66; unsplash.com: pp. 158–9 (John Towner), 7 bottom (VKI).

Michael D. Hill Jr, the copyright holder of the image on p. 49, Rcsmit, the copyright holder of the image on p. 216 and Roi Boshi, the copyright holder of the image on p. 88, have published the images online under conditions imposed by a Creative Commons Attribution ShareAlike 3.0 Generic license.

Readers are free:

- to share – to copy, distribute and transmit these last images alone
- to remix – to adapt these images alone

Under the following conditions:

- attribution – readers must attribute the images in the manner specified by the authors or licensers (but not in any way that suggests these parties endorse them or their use of the works).

Index